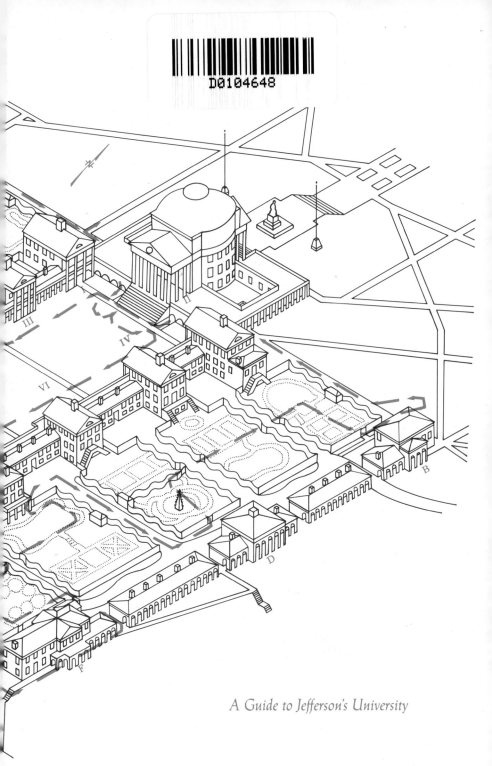

A Guide to Jefferson's University

THE

University Press of Virginia, Charlottesville

LAWN

A Guide to Jefferson's University

by PENDLETON HOGAN

photographs by BILL SUBLETTE

ACKNOW

THE UNIVERSITY PRESS OF VIRGINIA
Copyright © 1987 by the Rector and Visitors
of the University of Virginia

First published 1987
Second printing 1991

Book design by Janet Anderson using Trajanus type
designed by Warren Chappell, Artist-in-Residence
at the University of Virginia. Typesetting by
Graphic Composition, Inc.; printing and binding
by Thomson-Shore, Inc.

Library of Congress Cataloging-in-
Publication Data
Hogan, Pendleton
    The lawn: a guide to Jefferson's university.

    1. University of Virginia—Description—
Guidebooks.
I. Title.
LD5679.H66   1987   378.755'481
86–23330
ISBN 0–8139–1109–5

Printed in the United States of America

The first acknowledgment I can make
is to express my gratitude to Wilson
Walker Cowen, Director of the University Press of Virginia, whose idea this
book was.

I am indebted to the following
members of the University of Virginia
staff and faculty, in their several administrative and teaching capacities,
all of whom have been generous with
their knowledge, assistance, and advice: Raymond C. Bice, Jr., Secretary,
Board of Visitors, and Administrative
Assistant to the President; Alexander
G. Gilliam, Jr., Office of the President,
James E. Kinard, the University's History Officer, who patiently made available his broad knowledge of university
history; Irby B. Cauthen, Jr., Professor
of English; K. Edward Lay, Professor,
School of Architecture; Frederick D.
Nichols, Cary D. Langhorne Professor
of Architecture, Emeritus; J. Norwood
Bosserman, Professor of Architecture;
Murray Howard, Architect for the His-
toric Buildings and Grounds, and his
assistant, Clay S. Palazzo; Ernest H.
Ern, Vice President for Student Affairs;
Ernest C. Mead, Jr., Associate Professor
of Music; Thomas A. Mason, Associate

Editor, Papers of James Madison; Robert M. Hedrick, former Assistant Dean of Admissions; Alton C. Leake, Director, Physical Plant Operations; Larry G. Steward, Assistant Director for Landscape, Department of Buildings and Grounds; Charlotte Kohler, retired Editor of the *Virginia Quarterly Review*; Elizabeth Purvis, retired secretary to the Dean of the Graduate School of Arts and Sciences; and Evelyn W. Turnbull, Administrator, whose detailed knowledge of the Rotunda and its operations has been most helpful.

The staff of the University of Virginia Library has been extremely cooperative. In the Manuscripts Department, Anne Freudenberg, Michael F. Plunkett, Robert Hull, Gregory Johnson, and former employee Janet Linde have all helped. In the Reference Department, Roger Leachman, Gordon E. Hogg, and former employee Peter W. Farrell were equally cooperative, with the latter assisting for more than three years far beyond the call of duty. In the Fiske Kimball Fine Arts Library, Mary C. Dunnigan, Fine Arts Librarian, has provided essential help. Since at the start I was unacquainted with library personnel, the first person I consulted was Joan St. Clair Crane, Curator, American Literature, of the Rare Book Department, who guided me in the right direction. I am also indebted to the Division of Landscape Architecture for important details.

C. C. Wells of Charlottesville, a university alumnus, helped verify facts. Shortly before his death, Milton Grigg, architect and preservationist of historic properties, willingly answered questions and freely gave of his valuable knowledge of the Lawn. William Beiswanger of the Thomas Jefferson Memorial Foundation generously shared his knowledge of Jefferson as an architect.

I extend gratitude to Elizabeth Coles for typing. Finally, many members of the University Guide Service, throughout the entire time of preparation, have generously answered questions and shared their experiences as guides. I am grateful to them all.

Historical illustrations are from the Manuscripts Department of the University of Virginia Library.

PENDLETON HOGAN

CONTENTS

THE LAWN

A Guide to Jefferson's University

THE ROTUNDA

The University of Virginia welcomes visitors to its central grounds—the Lawn and the Ranges—of Thomas Jefferson's "academical village."

Student-guided tours begin at the Rotunda, the university's focal building and Jefferson's major architectural triumph. This guidebook also takes the Rotunda as its starting point. Finished in 1826, the Rotunda has long been considered one of the most distinguished buildings in America. A

brick walk of only several hundred feet leads to it from the bus stop at the chapel.

To the left is the university's interdenominational chapel, a neo-Gothic stone building designed by Charles E. Cassell of Baltimore. Its cornerstone was laid in 1885. On the right is one of Jefferson's brick serpentine walls, aesthetically pleasing and economical in that they are only one brick thick. Among the university's many noteworthy trees, a huge male Chinese gingko, planted about 1835, stands on the left between the chapel and the Rotunda. On this side of the Rotunda is the Shannon Garden, given by the faculty in 1978 to honor the presidency (1959–74) of Edgar Finley Shannon, Jr. This serene courtyard lies behind a colonnade of white plastered Tuscan columns in the style of those Jefferson used to flank the Lawn. The center brick pavement is surrounded by beds of liriope and shaded by magnolias.

Beyond the courtyard can be seen the original Flemish bond brick walls of the Rotunda, the centerpiece of Thomas Jefferson's university. Surrounding the building above its tiered windows is a wide white entablature and above this, under the edge of the dome's roof, is a narrow one.

On January 5, 1805, while serving as president of the United States, Jefferson wrote that a university should be not one big building but a village with a house for each professor and student rooms between, connected by a covered

passageway fronting on a court. Five years later he used the term "academical village." At the age of seventy-four, on a sultry July 18, 1817, he personally surveyed the land for an institution of higher learning. Here he laid out the grounds centered around a lawn; these terms are still in use today, for Jefferson seems never to have used the word *campus*. A year and a half later, on January 25, 1819, the Virginia General Assembly chartered and named the University of Virginia.

The entrance to the Rotunda is to the right and then left down the south passageway to the center door. To the left around the outside of the Rotunda are the twenty-four marble steps of the north portico, designed by Stanford

White of the New York architectural firm of McKim, Mead, and White after the disastrous fire of 1895. He also added the office wings and marble roof balustrades. A hedge of gigantic common boxwood frames the terrace below, and azaleas flank the broad walk out to University Avenue.

Centered in the plaza below the north portico is one of the university's three major statues of Jefferson. An imposing life-size figure in bronze, this monument by Moses Ezekiel was cast in Rome, erected in 1910, and bears the legend: "TO PERPETUATE THE TEACHINGS AND EXAMPLES OF THE FOUNDERS OF THE REPUBLIC, THIS MONUMENT TO THOMAS JEFFERSON WAS PRESENTED TO THE PEOPLE." It was presented to the university by the sculptor, who was born in Richmond in 1844. Standing on a bronze pedestal that is a replica of America's Liberty Bell, Jefferson is supported by four bronze winged female figures epitomizing four of the principles dearest to his heart: Liberty, facing north, Justice, facing south, Religious Freedom, west, and Human Freedom, east. The cluster rests on a red marble base, and the entire monument is about fifteen feet tall.

Across University Avenue to the far left is Carr's Hill, the residence of the university's president. This brick neoclassic house faced with a four-columned, pedimented portico was also designed by Stanford White and was built in 1907–9 on land bought in 1867. The hill had been the site of several mid-nineteenth-century dormitories, a portion of which still stands behind the house.

The columned red brick building next to Carr's Hill is Fayerweather Hall, designed by John Kevan Peebles of Norfolk. Built in 1893, it was the largest and most complete university gymnasium in the South. Now it houses the Department of Art. Directly across from the Rotunda is white-columned Madison Hall. Built by the college YMCA in 1904–5, it was bought by the university in October 1971 for the use of various university administrative offices including the Office of the President.

To the right near the Rotunda, the Victorian building is the Brooks Museum, which now houses a variety of offices. Designed by John R. Thomas of Rochester, New York, it was built in 1876–77. Between Brooks and the north portico of the Rotunda are several trees of note, including a *Paulownia tomentosa*, indigenous to Japan, which produces clusters of small orchidlike lavender flowers in the late spring. Nearby is a huge yulan magnolia which becomes a dome of white blossoms for a few days in March before its leaves appear. Its lower branches rest on the ground.

Jefferson did not plan a north portico, but when an expanding student body required more classroom space, an Annex was added in 1851–53 to the north of the Rotunda where the lower steps and terrace are now. Designed by Rob-

4

ert Mills, who received architectural training from Jefferson, it was connected to the Rotunda by a portico and contained a public hall seating 1,200, as well as classroom and laboratory space. The portico on its far side facing University Avenue was based on Jefferson's design for the south portico, but the columns were capped with cast-iron Corinthian capitals instead of carved Carrara marble ones. Student subscriptions permitted purchase for the Annex's hall of the university's first copy of Raphael's mural the *School of Athens*.

On a Sunday morning, October 27, 1895, a fire caused by faulty electrical wiring totally gutted both Annex and Rotunda. Of the latter, only its charred circular brick walls remained. A marble statue of Jefferson was saved, however, together with all portraits, some engineering and physics equipment, and about 15,000 books thrown from windows. The fire was so intense that when night came it was still burning. Bell Dunnington, the young daughter of a chemist on the university's faculty who lived a block away, wrote her sister the next morning: "Last night it looked as if the whole Rotunda was lit up from top to bottom. All the inside was bright, and the light shone out through the empty window frames just like it used to do at Commencement." Although the Rotunda was rebuilt, the Annex was not. In 1900 the present north portico was erected, and its marble Corinthian capitals were then carved in place matching those Jefferson had had carved in Italy for the south portico. All of the south portico capitals were so badly damaged that they had to be replaced with new ones.

On the east side of the Rotunda is another shaded courtyard. In it is the Darden Fountain, given by the university's professors and staff in 1960 to honor Colgate Whitehead Darden, Jr., governor of Virginia, 1942–46, and university president, 1947–59, "who loved and cherished these Grounds."

On the south side of the Rotunda are two long belowground open wings which housed Jefferson's gymnasia for student exercise. After the fire destroyed their wooden roofs and balustrades, Stanford White replaced these in concrete,

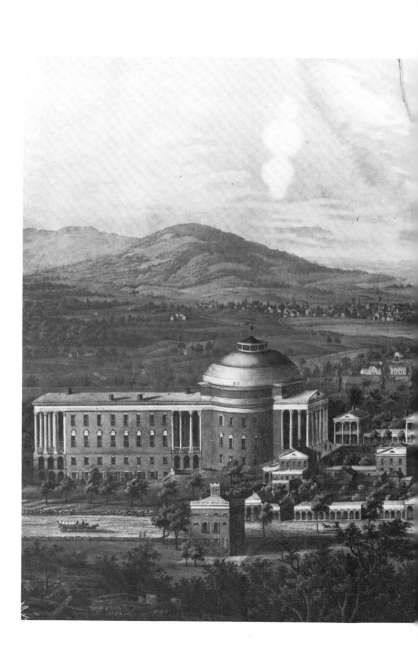

Bohn lithograph of 1856 showing the Annex

and in 1938–39 they were replaced in marble. The gymnasia's semicircular, or lunetted, windows with fanlight panes were one of Jefferson's favorite designs for small windows. He had seen them in France and England, used them at Monticello, and included many of them in the university buildings. The entrance to the Rotunda is in the middle of this passageway.

The ground-floor reception hall is in the shape of an hourglass. To simulate whitewash, as in Jefferson's days, the walls are covered with white water-base paint, and because the

ceilings are low, there are no crown moldings. Originally the ground level contained chemistry and natural science classrooms. The floors here, including hearths, are of handmade Albemarle County brick set in mortar in the herringbone style. None of the other Rotunda hearths are set in mortar.

Although the Rotunda holds much period furniture, the only household antique in the hall is the restored grandfather clock that belonged to William Barton Rogers, the university's third professor of natural philosophy, 1835–53. The entrance hall is lined with reproductions of the saddle-brown Windsor chairs that Jefferson wanted in the classrooms, with matching settees. At the far end of the hall is the university's bronze bell, ordered by Jefferson in 1825, the year before his death, and cast in Medway, Massachusetts, in 1827. One of Jefferson's requirements for the bell was that it must be heard across town, then two miles away. It hung in the south portico waking students at dawn until it cracked in 1886. After the fire, it was found in the rubble.

In 1817 when Jefferson was crystallizing his theories of higher education into specific plans, he requested suggestions from his friend Benjamin Henry Latrobe, the English-born professional architect then completing restoration of the U.S. Capitol in Washington after its wartime destruction by the British. Latrobe's sketch for the Lawn shows a dominant circular, domed building faced with a six-columned portico. Jefferson instantly adopted this idea.

Construction of the Rotunda began on October 7, 1822, and was completed in September 1826, shortly after Jefferson's death. For his specific model, he chose Rome's Pantheon, the classical temple to all the gods of Roman mythology. Jefferson had never seen the Pantheon, but he

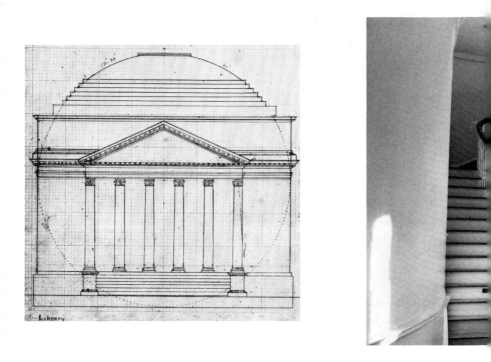

was an ardent admirer of the work of Andrea Palladio, the sixteenth-century Italian architect and interpreter of buildings that embodied the principles of early Rome. From his copy of Giacomo Leoni's 1721 edition of Palladio's *Four Books of Architecture*, Jefferson reduced the measurements of the Pantheon, decreased the front row of columns from eight to six, and added windows and steps. He thus scaled his brick temple down so that it would not dwarf the professors' brick houses, which he called "pavilions."

Jefferson believed that the heart of every academic institution is its repository of knowledge—its library—and that a library should be available at all times to everyone. Therefore, he designed and designated the Rotunda, the university's central building, as its library. With the books he initially selected in the Dome Room, the Rotunda served as the library for more than a century. The lower two floors con-

tained rooms to accommodate classes and other gatherings too large to be conducted in the pavilions.

After the fire of 1895, the Rotunda was restored in a monumental Beaux Arts mode, an eclectic interpretation of the ancient Roman style. Stanford White eliminated a floor of Jefferson's lecture rooms, widened the skylight in the dome, and created more shelf space for an expanding library around an open central area. The building remained thus for three-quarters of a century.

11

Then, in 1973, after twenty years of study sparked by Professor Frederick D. Nichols of the School of Architecture and carried out with the indispensable assistance of Francis L. Berkeley, Jr., restoration of the Rotunda to Jefferson's original design was begun. The project was financed by the Cary D. Langhorne Trust of Washington, D.C., and the U.S. Department of Housing and Urban Development. On April 13, 1976, the 233d anniversary of Jefferson's birth, the fully restored Rotunda was rededicated and is today what he once called it—"a sphere within a cylinder." In 1976, America's bicentennial year, the American Institute of Architects formally recognized Jefferson's university buildings as "the proudest achievement of American architecture since 1776."

The interiors of the ground floor and the main floor now have their original oval rooms and hourglass-shaped halls. The Dome Room, occupying the entire third floor, also was returned to Jefferson's incomparable design. Throughout the Rotunda enormous attention was paid to detail. The woodwork is painted with the same kind of lead-base paint used in Jefferson's time. The Rotunda's pine doors are "grained" in the nineteenth-century fashion—painted with a reddish base coat and a brown finishing layer that, before drying, is rubbed with rags and brushes to simulate rarer mahogany or walnut. Cornices in the five classical orders have been replaced as Jefferson had them. He based them on Leoni's edition of Palladio and on the 1766 edition of *Parallèle de l'architecture antique avec la moderne* by the French theorists Roland Fréart de Chambray and Charles Errard.

Instead of a single large staircase, Jefferson placed two double-curved staircases, unique in North America, against the solid brick walls. These were restored with their hand-carved black walnut railings. Their sweeping lines join the floors from ground level to Dome Room. On one upswinging curve there is a small landing with a miniature fireplace where students paused to warm their hands.

Although Jefferson's design has been restored, modernity has not been neglected. The electrical chandeliers are adapted from those of whale-oil days. Heating, cooling, and air circulation equipment is housed under the north portico steps and in the gable of the south portico. There are public restrooms in Jefferson's gymnasia. An elevator for the handicapped has been concealed in the space originally planned for clock weights. There is a pantry under the south portico's marble steps. The walls are veined with cables for electricity, telephones, and television, with controls hidden behind paneling. Air-conditioning vents are tucked inside moldings. The visitor sees none of this. The Rotunda appears today essentially as it was when it was built.

LOWER EAST OVAL ROOM

To the right on the ground floor is the lower east oval room. Over the fireplace hangs a reproduction of the first print of the academical village, engraved by Peter Maverick in 1822 from Jefferson's drawing. On the top margin of the print, Ellen Randolph Coolidge, Jefferson's granddaughter, made longhand notes of the pavilion facades. The Maverick Plan provided the public's first visual knowledge of the university. Copies were distributed to the General Assembly and then sold to prospective students for 50 cents. Although it includes the Rotunda with its south portico and flanking arcades, Jefferson acknowledged at the time that the "remaining building" had not been begun because of lack of funds. His task was further complicated by political and religious opposition to him and by aesthetic opposition to a round building. A second engraving, numbering the pavilions and the student rooms, was published in 1825.

To the left of the fireplace hangs a scaled rendering of the Roman Pantheon by C. F. Piranesi, dated 1787. In nearby cabinets are reprints of the 1776 edition of *The Buildings and Drawings of Andrea Palladio* by his pupil Vincenzo Scamozzi. Jefferson owned and used pattern books like these.

The Rotunda chimneys stand inside the building, so that they do not disrupt the building's cylindrical shape on the exterior. These fireplaces have never drawn well because their chimneys, in order not to be seen from the ground,

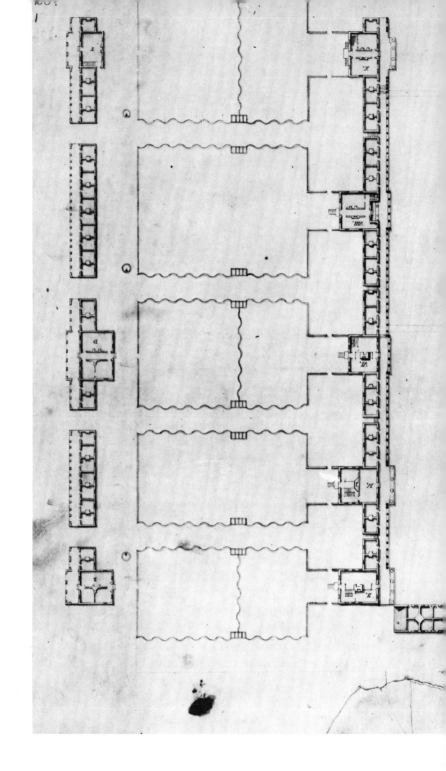

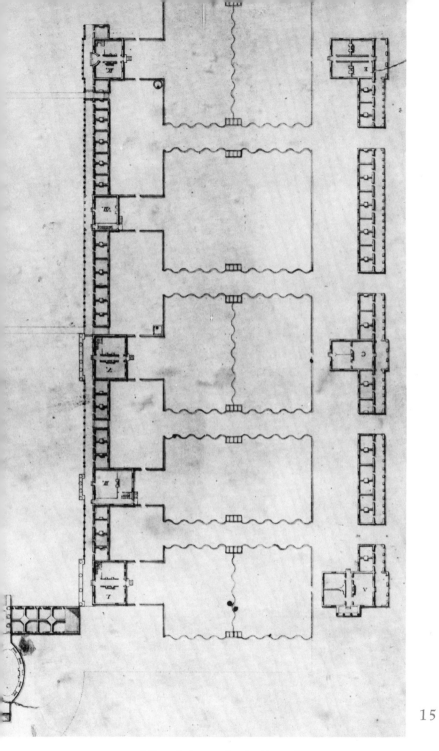

15

Jefferson's drawing for the Maverick engraving

project only six inches above the roof. On the Rotunda's exterior, blind windows cover all the chimneys to preserve uniformity. All rooms are uncurtained, and all the windows, including the false ones, are hung with wooden venetian blinds because records confirm Jefferson's order for them. From the outside, no one can detect the blanks.

When the Rotunda's walls were stripped to the brick during the restoration begun in 1973, two small ovens or grates with flues to the roof were discovered in this brick-floored room. It had been the chemistry laboratory. The ovens burned charcoal and were stoked from outside. Legend claims that these ovens once produced gunpowder for the Confederacy. In Virginia, the university, Hampden-Sydney College, founded in 1776, and Roanoke College at Salem managed to remain open throughout the four years of the War Between the States. After the first Battle of Manassas in 1861 and as the war continued to rage, the Rotunda, together with other buildings on the grounds, served as a military hospital.

This room contains photographs and cases of historic exhibits with self-explanatory labels. The oldest piece of furniture in the Rotunda, a French tall-case clock dating from the late seventeenth century, is here. On an easel stands an autographed photograph of Queen Elizabeth II and Prince Philip. Their Bicentennial visit on July 10, 1976, drew 18,000 persons to the Lawn.

LOWER WEST OVAL ROOM

Across the hall is an identical room, the lower west oval room. These rooms are now lighted with electrified reproduction whale-oil lanterns. In addition to an American Empire mahogany sideboard and a walnut Sheraton dining table made in Scotland in 1826, the west oval room contains a grained pine storage cupboard used by Professor Rogers. A reproduction of the Joshua Fry–Peter Jefferson map of Virginia and Maryland drawn in 1751 hangs over the fireplace.

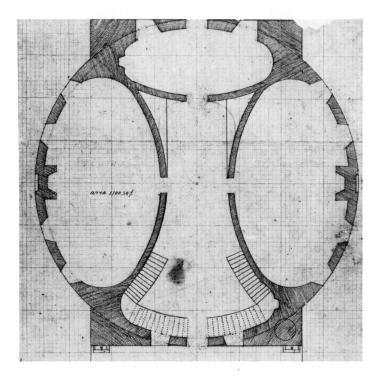

Fry and Peter Jefferson, Thomas's father, were the first to chart Virginia as far west as the Blue Ridge Mountains. On a windowsill stands part of an original capital from a south portico column, one of those carved in Italy for Jefferson, recovered after the fire. A reproduction of the 1825 Maverick Plan stands on an easel.

LOWER NORTH OVAL ROOM

The lower north oval room houses a small conference room.

MAIN-FLOOR ENTRANCE HALL

Upon special occasions, the south portico's double inside glass doors are opened to receive dignitaries directly into the upper entrance hall. In each room of this floor Jefferson

placed a different classical cornice, and the hall's deep, layered crown molding is in the plain Tuscan order. Dominating the hall is the life-size white marble statue of Jefferson daringly saved from the 1895 fire. Carved by Alexander Galt, a Norfolk sculptor trained in Italy, this statue was commissioned by the Virginia General Assembly in 1854. Because of the war, it was not unveiled until July 1, 1868, in the Dome Room. Persons who had known Jefferson in life confirmed the statue's authenticity, stating it "is Jefferson himself." His grandchildren considered it his best likeness.

When the fire struck, the statue still stood in the Dome Room. Despite its overpowering weight, a group of students maneuvered it on a mattress to the western stairs while fire raged in the Annex. They worked it down the staircase, feet foremost, until they got it onto the south portico and down to the Lawn just as the Rotunda became an inferno. The statue suffered virtually no damage. Today a secret group known as the Seven Society is said to collect mail at the statue. The Sevens' insignia appears on walls and steps about the grounds, as do those of the IMP and Z societies.

All floors in the Rotunda's upper stories gleam with the patina of old pine. Some of these yellow heart pine floorboards were taken from early nineteenth-century Virginia buildings, while others are from old beams that were quartersawn as Jefferson had insisted to expose a grain unlikely to warp. Some of the brass locks on the Rotunda doors are antique, and others are reproductions made in England. The five chandeliers in the three oval rooms on this floor are in the Argand style that Jefferson liked. They were made from the molds for the chandeliers in the old U.S. House of Representatives Chamber in the Capitol at Washington.

MAIN-FLOOR EAST OVAL ROOM

This stately room, originally a classroom, is the meeting chamber of the university's governing body, its Board of Visitors, of which Jefferson was the first rector. The term *visitor* was borrowed from the College of William and Mary, his alma mater.

The gigantic mahogany conference table in the Duncan Phyfe style was built for the room in 1976 in Harrisonburg by Virginia craftsmen. The rug was woven in India for the room.

The standing portrait of Jefferson over the mantel, one of the few full-length portraits for which he posed, shows him in his study at Monticello. It was painted by Bass Otis in 1818. This was the year the Virginia Assembly was finally persuaded to appropriate $15,000 to found a state university. It also authorized what came to be known as the Rockfish Gap Commission, to which the governor appointed members. With Jefferson as chairman and James Madison a member, the commission was to select a site, choose plans, and work out operations; after much discussion, it confirmed the project Jefferson already had underway at Charlottesville.

The frieze in this room is in the Corinthian order, taken

from the Roman Baths of Caracalla. Its acanthus leaves and rosettes honor the beauty of nature, and its egg-and-dart motif, used by the ancient Greeks, symbolizes both life and death. The design of the mantel here and in the room across the hall, with strong dentils, is one that Jefferson used throughout the pavilions.

Against the inside wall, underneath antique bull's-eye convex mirrors, is a pair of late nineteenth-century rosewood mirror-backed wall tables. The pedestals are carved and gilded wooden eagles.

MAIN-FLOOR WEST OVAL ROOM

This elegant salon, furnished with fine pieces of its period, is the official reception room for the university. This room, once used for classes in the arts and letters, is now the setting for occasions of special significance and the reception of distinguished visitors. Its highly distinctive Doric crown molding, adapted from the Baths of Diocletian in Rome, features the face of the Roman sun god. Before the fireplace is a small Persian rug, in red and blue, that was a Bicentennial gift from the empress of Iran.

Above the mantel hangs one of the three 1821 portraits of Jefferson by Thomas Sully, painted from life when the subject was seventy-eight and at his busiest building the university. This small portrait, accentuated by a dark shadow box, clearly shows remaining evidence of his sandy hair along with the white. On the mantel stand three still functional antique Argand lamps that burn whale oil. Jefferson brought several such fixtures back from Paris in 1789 and, because they gave a better light and were more economical than candles, promoted their use.

Facing each other are two Phyfe-period sofas in green brocade. The one on the left, though reconstructed, is attributed to Duncan Phyfe's shop, and its carved crest rail to Phyfe's own hand. The front legs of this piece are carved

acanthus leaves topped with Ionic capitals. The front legs of the other sofa are carved griffins.

Centered before the fireplace is a large American Empire mahogany library table, while flanking the fireplace is a matching pair of Empire petticoat tables with white marble front legs set in ormolu. Against the inside wall stand a nineteenth-century American Empire desk-bookcase and an American Hepplewhite gentleman's mahogany breakfront of about 1810.

MAIN-FLOOR NORTH OVAL ROOM

As in the early days, classes, lectures, examinations, and conferences are conducted in this room. Because the most decorative item here is the unglazed Sèvres porcelain bust of the marquis de Lafayette, it is often called the Lafayette Room. The bust, a copy of the original by the French sculptor Jean-Antoine Houdon, was donated to the university in 1904 by the Government of France. It commemorates the deep personal friendship of the French patriot-general, who fought in the American Revolution, and Jefferson. It is a constant reminder of Lafayette's visit in 1824 when he became the unfinished Rotunda's first official visitor.

The Ionic frieze depicts both human and animal life by featuring cherubs and ox skulls, honored with decorative garlands. It is taken from the ancient Temple of Fortuna Virilis in Rome, shown in the 1721 edition of Palladio. The mantel is a scaled-down version of the others on this floor.

On the outside wall hangs the 1833 three-panel Herman Böÿe–Henry S. Tanner map of Virginia, including what is now West Virginia. This map is especially interesting because the scenes depicted in the cartouches are all associated with Jefferson. On the left, Benjamin Tanner's 1827 engraving of the university shows the three terraces and the roof scheme of the pavilion parapets as Jefferson designed them. In the center cartouche is the Natural Bridge, which he once owned. On the right, the Tanner engraving of Richmond featuring Jefferson's State Capitol is so precise that individual buildings are visible.

THE DOME ROOM

The Dome Room on the third floor of the Rotunda is the most impressive feature in Jefferson's academical village.

In its unadorned simplicity, this white circular chamber with its ring of fifteen-foot double columns and two rings of galleries intended to hold the books forming the university's library has been called one of the most beautiful rooms in America. Its classical capitals, railings, and moldings are in white and pale gray. Daylight pours in around the circle and down from the round center skylight long known as Jefferson's "oculus."

Having used four classical orders to decorate the rooms below, as derived by the Romans from the still more ancient Greeks, Jefferson realized the culmination of his taste when he styled the Dome Room in the Composite order of Palladio. Thus, he brought indoors the same lines he used in the two white Composite entablatures—one broad, one narrow—on the outside of the Rotunda.

Because in everything he created Jefferson based his guiding principles on logic and reason, it was inevitable that he would place a Temple of Knowledge at his university's center. With the library in the Dome Room, he stated his unshakable belief that learning and teaching are essential to man's creative being. Only two years before he died, he made a list of almost seven thousand volumes to be acquired for the University's original library.

He further envisioned the Dome Room with its ceiling painted sky-blue and gilt stars in their proper celestial positions, and he designed a movable seat from which the operator could place and move every star. Never implemented, this idea would have given America its first planetarium. His oculus was built, however, of glass and wood. Restoration researchers found an order for three replacement panes of glass and from these learned that Jefferson's skylight had been supported on a wooden frame with spokes radiating from a central wooden axis. This device leaked, despite various alterations in the nineteenth century. The 1976 skylight of glass and aluminum gives the same effect as Jefferson's and is guaranteed not to leak. Further, the ceiling has been acoustically treated with perforated aluminum panels that absorb reverberation of sound. As before the fire, the room is again used for lectures, banquets, and chamber music concerts.

The room's one and one-half story columns replace Stanford White's two-and one-half story ones, and to help carry the dome, a steel support has been concealed in every second pillar. Although Jefferson's capitals were of black locust, today's are plaster; they were less expensive to produce, do not split, and are easier to repair.

Although no photographs appear to exist of the rooms below, early photographic views materially aided in restoring the Dome Room. One showed the floorboards laid straight across to connect the facing fireplaces. For his original floors, Jefferson specified pine from trees grown in stated latitudes, to preclude wood too burled or too soft; these floors duplicate those, and they are underlined with acoustical material to help deaden sound.

The university's library was moved to Alderman Library in 1938 and has been further expanded, but the Dome Room still houses a selection of books in cases rebuilt to Jefferson's arrangement. So cleverly did he fan them out behind the columns that from the center of the room not a book is visible. Also behind the columns, between the bookcases, are study alcoves.

Over the east mantel hangs an oil portrait of General John

Hartwell Cocke, a member of the first Board of Visitors, whose home, Bremo, one of Jefferson's builders, John Neilson, helped design. In early administrative matters, Cocke was of inestimable help to Jefferson and Madison. Over the west mantel hangs the 1775 edition of the Fry-Jefferson map.

Visitors using the stairs to and from the Dome Room little realize they are polishing the walnut railings as their hands pass over them. No other polish is used. Against the unthinkable event of another fire, in addition to sprinklers throughout the Rotunda, a remarkable "deluge system" would throw a curtain of water around the stairs to assure evacuation.

Of all events ever held in the Dome Room, two are truly memorable. On November 5, 1824, at 3:00 P.M., Albemarle County citizens gave a three-hour grand banquet to honor the marquis de Lafayette, then on a state visit to America. Legend says 400 men sat, while ladies dined on the Lawn and in the pavilions. The Charlottesville *Central Gazette* of November 10, 1824, reported that the guests were arranged "in three concentric circles," with Jefferson on Lafayette's right, and Madison, soon to become the university's second rector, on Jefferson's right. When toasted, Jefferson was emotionally unable to respond. His reply was read, while Lafayette grasped his hand and sobbed aloud.

In America's Bicentennial year, on July 10, 1976, the governor of Virginia, Mills E. Godwin, Jr., gave a luncheon in the Dome Room for Queen Elizabeth II and Prince Philip. The queen addressed the largest assemblage to date on the Lawn, mentioning "my kinsman, George Washington," and then progressed to the Rotunda. Seated under the dome in soft daylight, Her Majesty was unaware that only the day before pie-shaped pieces of white butcher paper had been pasted to the top side of Jefferson's skylight to keep the blazing midday sun out of her eyes.

A century and a half earlier, in June 1826, a few weeks before his death, the eighty-three-year-old Jefferson rode his horse Eagle from Monticello to the Rotunda on his last visit to the university he had created. At the top of the Dome Room stairs, he looked out the center window over the Lawn. Beyond Pavilions IX and X lay open country. Below, workmen were lifting the first marble Corinthian capital, which he had long awaited from Italy, to the south portico's southwest corner column. William Wertenbaker, a student appointed librarian in April, brought a chair, and Jefferson sat for an hour watching. When the capital was in place, he rose, descended the stairs, mounted his horse, and rode away.

THE LAWN

Outside the Rotunda, the south portico overlooks the Lawn. It is not apparent to the eye that its Corinthian capitals were replaced after the fire. With his characteristic thoroughness, when Jefferson ordered the university bell he also ordered an exterior clock for the Rotunda. This too was lost in the fire and was replaced with one mechanism for clocks in both porticoes, a gift in 1899 from Jefferson M. Levy of New York, who then owned Monticello. Up the south portico's fifteen marble steps and to the right of the door are bronze plaques in memory of those students and alumni who lost their lives in the military service of the Confederacy and those who gave their lives for freedom in "The World War." To the left of the door, a bronze marker commemorates Woodrow Wilson's two years, 1879–81, as a student at the university.

From the south portico Jefferson's long green Lawn stretches to the south, covering nearly two acres. It is bounded east and west by parallel rows of five two-story pavilions. These are connected by one-story colonnades—white plastered columns in the simple Tuscan order—behind which are fifty-four student rooms, twenty-six (even nos. 2–52) on the East Lawn and twenty-eight (odd nos. 1–55) on the West Lawn. Rooms on the Lawn are reserved for fourth-year student leaders who, based on their service to the university, are voted into them by their peers.

In promoting man's right to the widest possible dissemination of knowledge, Jefferson based his concept of the university on the ancient Greek practice of gathering students about a teacher in a room or glade. He broadened this arrangement by placing professors to live among their students. Adding a reliance on student self-government, he hoped to create a climate for the individual's right to the "pursuit of happiness." Few of his contemporaries believed that this radical plan could possibly succeed.

In the pavilions the early professors lived upstairs and taught in a room on the main floor open to the Lawn. Grad-

ually, however, as their families and requirements for living space increased, and as the student body grew, classes were moved from the pavilions into the Rotunda. When it was outgrown in the mid-nineteenth century, they were moved into the Annex. After the fire of 1895, classes were moved again, into three large new buildings at the south end of the Lawn.

The flat-seamed metal roofs of the colonnades that front the pavilions and the student rooms still provide two upper walkways linking the pavilions, one on each side of the Lawn. The walkways are bordered on the outside with Chinese trellis railings in Jefferson's design. All the pavilions except No. VII—the faculty club called the Colonnade Club—are faculty residences. Behind them are shady walled gardens where faculty and students relax, as Jefferson intended, and visitors

may stroll. Here the serpentine walls cast undulating shadows across the many garden paths and walkways.

When the university opened on a windy March 7, 1825, the trees on the Lawn could not have been more than two years old. Over a year and a half before the university was chartered, at the Board of Visitors' first regular meeting on May 5, 1817, Jefferson's plan for the institution was approved. Five days later he wrote Dr. William Thornton, architect for the national Capitol, requesting suggestions for

buildings. Within his letter he drew a rough sketch of a quadrangle open on one side, with pavilions and student rooms behind colonnades and an open lawn in the center. Across the lawn he wrote, "grass and trees." A month later, on June 12, he sent a similar letter to Benjamin Henry Latrobe again with a tentative sketch and the words "grass and trees." After Jefferson surveyed the site on July 18, using his theodolite, locust stakes, and twine, the land was graded and the terraces were leveled for grass.

In 1823, when all the buildings around the Lawn except the Rotunda had been erected, the university proctor, Arthur S. Brockenbrough, paid $1.50 to Mary Gardner for 100 young locust trees. Seven years later Professor John A. G. Davis arrived at the university and "found the double row of young locust trees, which had been planted on each side of the Lawn, which were giving promise of shade in years to come." The earliest prints of the Lawn, 1827, 1828, and 1831, show no trees probably because they were too small to be impressive, while the lack of trees in the 1837 and 1845

Benjamin Tanner's 1827 engraving

prints suggests that they were left out to display the buildings fully. Until late in the twentieth century, as trees died they were replaced with varying species; today they are generally replaced with ash trees.

Some 300 feet behind the pavilions on both sides of the Lawn are parallel rows of student rooms called East and West Range. Jefferson faced the Ranges with brick arcades instead of colonnades and included in each Range three buildings to serve as student refectories, or dining halls. These he called Hotels A, B, C, D, E, and F. Long outgrown, these small buildings in general are used for offices and faculty residences. There are fifty-four student rooms in the Ranges. Except for Edgar Allan Poe's room at 13 West Range, all are occupied, generally by graduate students chosen by lottery.

All Lawn buildings are of red brick in the Federal style. The pavilions vary in size and detail; Pavilion VII, measuring approximately 35 feet in width by 27 feet 6 inches in depth, was originally the smallest, while Pavilion III, measuring approximately 37 feet 6 inches in width by 42 feet 6 inches in depth, was originally the largest. For many years their exterior trim has been white with the trim of the student rooms a sand-pebbled putty color. Until the 1980s all doors and window shutters, except the Rotunda's white doors and the upper and lower white doors of Pavilion VII, were in traditional Virginia bottle-green paint. In 1986, after detailed architectural research and paint analysis, the doors and shutters of Pavilion VIII were repainted in what is now believed to have been their original colors. This research is being continued on other pavilions. As in the Rotunda's upper rooms, Jefferson used a different classical order for each pavilion's facade so that all could serve as constantly available subjects for architectural study.

When Jefferson and other Visitors bought the land in 1817, they took what was available, knowing it contained a rocky ridge from north to south. The Rotunda rests on the ridge's peak, and it was the ridge that necessitated laying out the Lawn in three terraces, each 200 feet wide but of varying lengths. The fourth tier was added when the Lawn's south end was enclosed after the fire to provide needed classroom space.

Although Jefferson never anticipated shutting off the view with buildings at the Lawn's south end, he did plan a botanical garden down the hillside there. Of about six acres, it was to be enclosed in a serpentine wall seven feet high. Aside from its beauty, it would have provided constant seasonal specimens for botanical study. In May 1826 Jefferson and Dr. John Patton Emmet, professor of natural history and chemistry, selected the garden site, but because Jefferson died less than two months later it was never planted.

Shortly after buying the land, Jefferson had a brickyard set up west of West Range, near where the anatomical building would be placed in 1826 and where Alderman Library now stands. It was adjacent to a large spring that fed a pond below the present library where students ice-skated during the rare prolonged cold spells. Brick production was slow. Virginia's red clay was dug, weathered all winter in heaps on the ground, and in the spring mixed with water and sand. Handmade brick molds of hard wood, bound with iron for strength, were filled by hand. After natural drying, the bricks were kiln-fired. Even though Jefferson at times personally supervised the brickmaking and at its peak 180,000 were turned out in one month, not enough bricks were produced; 300,000 had to be bought locally from John Perry.

Jefferson had the facades of the pavilions and hotels laid in Flemish bond, with its alternating stretchers and headers. The sides and rears of Lawn buildings and some of the student rooms were done in variations of the common bond; similar variations appear below the water tables. The abutting lines in certain walls show that the Lawn buildings were erected separately during the years 1817 to 1822 as money became available, not in one continuous process.

As the visitor stands at the south portico of the Rotunda during the winter when the trees are bare, a glance down one side of the Lawn and up the other shows that all ten pavilions are rectangular buildings behind columns. The five pavilions of East Lawn, to the left, were designed by Jefferson in fifteen days in 1819 at age seventy-six—a remarkable accomplishment. At that time, work was progressing on the five West Lawn pavilions. His objective was "to create a small and separate lodge for each professorship," with style.

During Jefferson's five years in Europe (1784–89), he became enamored of two buildings in France whose influence is reflected on the Lawn. One was the Maison Carrée, the ancient Roman temple at Nîmes. When asked in 1785 for

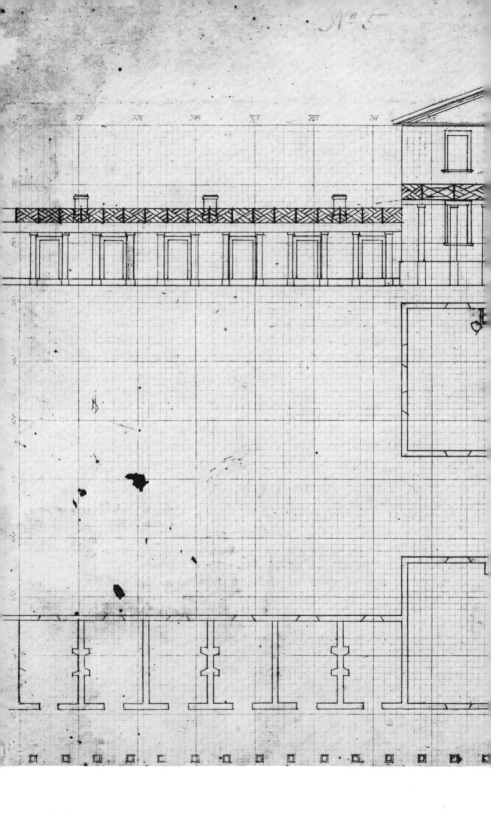

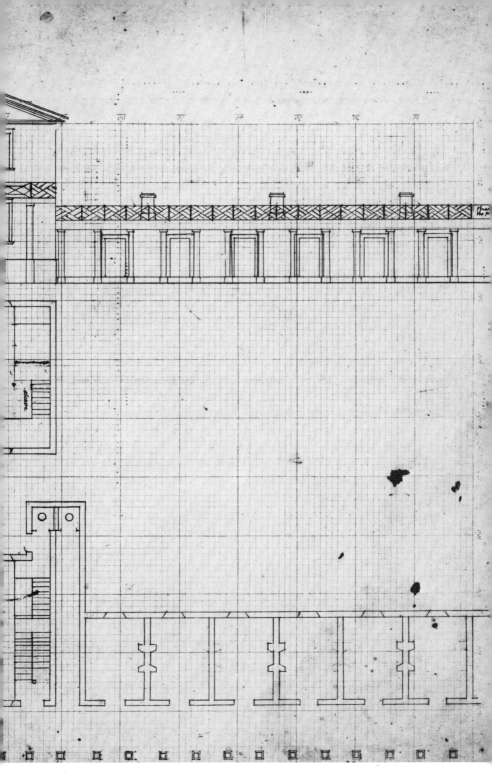

An early study by Jefferson for Pavilion VII and student rooms

ideas for a Virginia state capitol, he sent to Richmond plans and a plaster model of this rectangular, pedimented, columned temple. Later he carried some of these lines into residential architecture. Although all ten pavilions vary from each other, in the style of the Maison Carrée Jefferson gave seven of them porticoes with two-story columns. He fronted all the pavilions with upper galleries. But despite basic similarities, a large part of the pavilions' charm lies in their differences.

The other building that directly influenced Jefferson was the Hôtel de Salm, a magnificent town house in Paris that he watched being built. This columned mansion, now the Palais de la Legion d'Honneur, a superb example of the neoclassical fashion, balances grace and mass and was partly responsible for Jefferson's lasting infatuation with two-story houses built to look like one-story houses. His use of floor-length windows in some pavilions is reminiscent of the Hôtel de Salm, and the interior court of this French house could have influenced the colonnaded Lawn. Other precedents for Jefferson's grand plan have been suggested, including the Salines Royales of the French architect Claude-Nicolas Ledoux and Louis XVI's favorite chateau at Marly, which Jefferson visited while in France. There the king's pavilion was an axis, and six separate pavilions formed a row on both sides of a wide expanse of grass, one for each of the twelve months. At the Certosa di Pavia, the ancient Carthusian monastery in northern Italy that he visited in 1787, Jefferson saw still another grouping of buildings that may have contributed to his plans for his academical village. At the Certosa, one side of a grand cloister is filled by the church and ducal palace while the other three sides are bordered by twenty-four arcaded cells for the monks, each a little three-room house with a garden.

Although Roman villas did not have chimneys, Jefferson gave each pavilion one center chimney containing all the flues to conserve heat. Except for Nos. III and IV, the pavilions have been extended rearward over the years, and several now have additional chimneys. Four of the pavilions and the

Rotunda's two porticoes have the newly introduced metal roofs with stand-up seams that Jefferson considered the longest-lasting roof and taught the workmen how to install. Originally, all of the pavilions had basement kitchens.

Before the pavilions were built, Jefferson planned each as a separate school, or department, to be presided over by a professor who would live above his classroom. Jefferson wanted all "sciences," all useful branches of human knowledge, taught in the highest degree to which the human mind had carried them. Instead of a fixed curriculum, he set up an elective system that permitted each student to choose his own subjects. A student could enroll in more than one school but was not required to do so. He must, however, register and pay for one year. The first session in 1825 ran for ten and one-half months. Although lectures were not then customary, Jefferson wanted them given.

He drew up a schedule of classes before there was a faculty to conduct them. In its August 1818 report to the General Assembly, drafted by Jefferson, the Rockfish Gap Commission included a "tabular statement of the branches of learning" to be taught in the university. The ancient languages were Latin, Greek, and Hebrew, and the modern languages were French, Spanish, Italian, German, and Anglo-Saxon. Pure mathematics embraced algebra, fluxions, elementary and transcendental geometry, and both naval and military architecture. Physico-mathematics covered eight subjects: mechanics, statics, dynamics, pneumatics, acoustics, optics, astronomy, and geography. One branch was physics, or natural philosophy; and another included chemistry, mineralogy, botany, zoology, anatomy, and medicine. Another field encompassed government, political economy, the law of nature and nations, municipal law, and history. And not forgotten was the branch that included ideology, general grammar, ethics, rhetoric, belles lettres, and the fine arts.

Construction began with Pavilion VII in 1817. Funds were scarce and work was slow. Without the sage advice, tact, and loyal persistence of Joseph Carrington Cabell in pressing for funds in the Virginia Senate, Jefferson never could have re-

alized his dream of founding the university. The scholarly Cabell, who was thirty-five years younger than Jefferson, served on the Board of Visitors from 1819 until his death in 1856 and was the university's third and fifth rector. In 1828 it was stated publicly in the Virginia Senate that in establishing the university Cabell was "second only to Jefferson."

On September 30, 1821, Jefferson wrote General Cocke: "Pavilions Number 3 and 7, undertaken in 1817 and 1818, Numbers 2, 4, 5, and 9 finished. 17 marble caps from Italy [for] No. 2, 3, 5, 8. No. 1, 6, 8, and 10 not finished." By October 7, 1822, the ten pavilions, the 109 student rooms, and the six hotels were considered completed. Today there are only 108 student rooms, for No. 56 East Range was re-

moved when Levering Hall was built abutting Hotel F. In 1822 some plastering remained to be done, and the final capitals for the columns still had not arrived from Italy. The gardens had not been entirely laid out, nor had the serpentine walls, intended to prevent intrusion, been erected. One year later, in October 1823, all buildings except the Rotunda were ready for occupancy. Now a faculty was needed.

When Jefferson found that his personal efforts to secure professors in the United States were unproductive, he dispatched, on May 8, 1824, his newly selected professor of law, thirty-three-year-old Francis Walker Gilmer, to Britain. Gilmer's assignment was to locate and sign professors on five-year contracts for the various chairs, or schools, and to buy

41

books and apparatus. Public criticism of the empty pavilions was mounting. Facing reality, the Visitors reduced the number of professors sought from ten to eight. Gilmer finally signed five for salaries of no less than $1,000 per year nor more than $1,500, plus the modest fee each student would pay his professor.

One of the five secured was German born, the others British. By the spring of 1825 three more professors, all American citizens, had been found. The first two Europeans arrived separately in December 1824 and the remaining three early in 1825. Three brought their wives, while two were then unmarried. The pavilions had been habitable for several years but were devoid of furnishings. Today, professors who live in the pavilions still provide most of their own furniture. The pavilions are assigned by seniority, and the prestige of living on the Lawn, for professors and students alike, is enormous.

All of the 108 original student rooms are located at ground level. Fifty-four, behind the roofed colonnades adjacent to the pavilions, face on the Lawn. There are twenty-seven rooms in each of the arcaded Ranges, all facing outward. Of red brick, all student quarters are one-story separate rooms measuring 12 feet 6 inches square. Each room has one door with louvered blinds and, opposite in its rear wall, one window for light and cross ventilation. All rooms except No. 50 on the East Lawn, for which there was insufficient space, have usable fireplaces; they are on inside walls back to back, so that one chimney with two flues serves two adjacent rooms. The student rooms have central heat now, but every autumn stacks of firewood appear outside many of the doors. All rooms except Poe's are fitted with clothes cupboards instead of the original wall pegs and with washbasins having hot and cold water. Bathrooms are outside, on the basement level.

On April 7, 1824, the Board of Visitors set tuition, payable in advance by each student directly to each professor, at $50 for attendance in one class for the ten and one-half month session. For two classes each student paid $60, each professor receiving $30, and for three classes each paid $75, with each professor receiving $25. Students were expected to attend the classes of three professors. At their October 4 meeting the Visitors decided that no student under sixteen would be admitted and that student rooms were to be occupied by "two students each and no more," at $15 yearly rent to be

paid one-half by each occupant. If a student wished to occupy a room alone, as Edgar Allan Poe did, he paid the full fee. In addition, each student paid $15 for use of the university's "public apartments" and made his own arrangements with hotelkeepers. No keeper was permitted to charge more than $100 per student for board for the ten and one-half month session. This fee included room maintenance.

On October 7, 1826, the Visitors determined that the proctor would inspect "the furnishments" of student rooms "at least once a month." Later, this became once a week. Since about 1960 rooms have been allotted singly. During

the early years of low enrollment, these student rooms were often put to other uses, such as faculty studies. When the proctor moved into Hotel D in 1827, he was allowed the room next door, at 22 East Range, as his office. Later, this room became the university post office.

Jefferson accentuated the perspective effects on the Lawn when he graded the natural fall of the land into level terraces. Knowing that the farther an object is from the viewer the smaller it appears, and that the same is true for spaces, he progressively increased the distance between pavilions from the Rotunda by placing four student rooms between Nos. II and IV, six between Nos. IV and VI, seven between Nos. VI and VIII, and eight between Nos. VIII and X, with one on the south side of Pavilion X.

In distance, the West Lawn Pavilions I and III and the East Lawn Pavilions II and IV are spaced 89 feet 8½ inches on centers; Nos. III and V and Nos. IV and VI are spaced 126

feet 4½ inches on centers; Nos. V and VII and Nos. VI and VIII are spaced 143 feet 6 inches on centers; and Nos. VII and IX and Nos. VIII and X are spaced 157 feet 1 inch on centers. As is clear on the Maverick Plan, the south pavilion gardens are fifty feet wider than those at the north. Even the wooden railings above the colonnades are slightly higher toward the south, thus creating the appearance of being the same size all the way.

From the Rotunda's south portico, the visual effect is that the parallel lines of the buildings framing the Lawn are widening and that the pavilions are equally spaced. This false perspective is an optical illusion. From the south looking northward, the perspective effects are in reverse. The diminishing space between pavilions seems to draw the parallel lines closer, so that they appear to be converging in the distance as do railway tracks. This focuses vision directly on the Rotunda, the university's centerpiece.

EAST LAWN

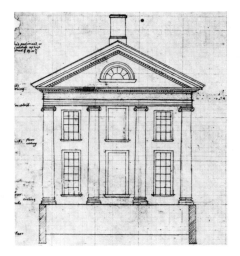

PAVILION II

To the left from the south portico of the Rotunda is a typical example of the continuity in Jefferson's design. The windows of the Rotunda's underground passageway repeat the same fanlight pattern he used for the semicircular window in the tympanum of Pavilion II's pediment. Further, by also using this fanlight, one of several on the Lawn, in the rectangular transom over the pavilion's double front doors, he gave the house symmetry.

With its three-bay temple front, Pavilion II is an excellent example of the Roman Revival style. For its facade, Jefferson chose the Ionic order from Palladio, as used in the Temple of Fortuna Virilis in Rome. The frieze on the building's front fascia contains the same elements—the cherub, the ox skull, and the linking decorative garland—in the cornice of the Rotunda's north oval room. With a plain fascia and egg-and-dart molding over dentils, its ornamentation continues around the building. Although it was completed by October

1822, the first professor did not move into Pavilion II until 1827, when the teaching of anatomy and surgery began.

In this pavilion, as well as others, Jefferson stressed the vertical by placing the gallery door directly over the front door and the upper front windows directly over the lower ones. From a distance, this fenestration creates the impression of very tall openings, accented by a wide cross molding—actually the gallery's Chinese trellis railing.

Pavilion II's white two-story columns of plastered brick are set forward, for emphasis, from the front of the colonnade. The Ionic capitals were among the first seventeen received from Italy and are of Carrara marble. The three eggs, separated by darts, between the volutes are crisply carved, and the two corner volutes point outward.

Only from under the gallery is it clear that the columns are freestanding. Contrary to usual design, they do not support the gallery; there is an intentional gap of some four inches between its edge and the columns. Supporting the gallery are four thin iron tie-rods suspended from the pediment downward to the gallery floor. Jefferson was one of the

47

first American builders to use metal suspension rods, and all seven pavilions with two-story porticoes have them. He carefully placed these rods behind the columns so that they are not seen from the front.

Pavilion II retains all ten of its original front window and door blind holdbacks. These are of handwrought iron fitted into the brick wall and vary in size and thickness. When vertical, they resemble the letter J. Whether Jefferson realized that the functional shape also formed his initial is unknown, but they were installed for the front blinds on all the pavilions.

The first occupant of Pavilion II was Dr. John Patton Emmet, professor of natural history and chemistry, who soon moved across the Lawn to Pavilion I. For a time after Jefferson's death, members of the Board of Visitors lodged in Pavilion II when they met at the university. Its first permanent resident was Thomas Johnson, demonstrator in anatomy and surgery in 1827–31 and professor in 1831–34. Its longest continuous resident was a nephew of Joseph C. Cabell, Dr. James L. Cabell, professor of anatomy and surgery, who lived here for fifty-three years.

Pavilion II survived the Rotunda fire of 1895 only with help from a bucket brigade which kept wet blankets on its north wall and window trim. Along the colonnaded passageway, the white tooled joints in the brickwork can be seen. The offset where Pavilion II and student room No. 2 join shows that they are separate structures built at different times.

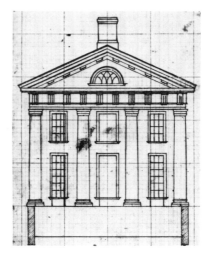

PAVILION IV

The four student rooms between Pavilions II and IV are divided in the center by steps leading down to Rotunda Alley between the gardens behind the pavilions.

In his notes for the classical order decorating Pavilion IV, Jefferson stated that he would use the "Doric of Albano from Chambray." As his drawing for this pavilion with its three-bay temple front shows, the door was first in the center,

under the gallery door. After classes were moved to the Rotunda and the first floor became part of the residential quarters, the movement of an inside wall necessitated moving the door to the left. Because in Pavilion IV and five other pavilions Jefferson placed the same floor-length, triple-sash windows he had used at Monticello, the door of Pavilion IV could be moved to an existing opening of the same dimensions. The door is distinguished by a brass escutcheon of later date bearing Jefferson's head in profile. These triple-sash windows, sometimes called "walk-out" windows, admit light all the way to the floor and, when the top sash is lowered and the bottom is raised, provide the best possible air circulation.

The muntins in Pavilion IV's pediment window are in a multiple-arch pattern, and the same design appears in the doorway's transom. The white-painted Doric columns are well proportioned; their concrete bases and capitals were molded in Charlottesville. Both the triglyphs in the wide frieze and the paneled, louvered blinds contribute to the balanced verticality of the building's front. Two contrasting patterns are used in the Chinese trellis railing of the gallery, while across the bottom sash of the first-floor windows another railing repeats one of these.

Initially, all pavilions were assigned by lot, and the first occupants of Pavilion IV were controversial, irascible George Blaettermann and his English wife. Born in Saxony in 1782, at forty-three the oldest of the first professors, he arrived in January 1825 and was given the chair of modern languages. A brilliant linguist, he was able to teach nine languages, including Dutch and Anglo-Saxon. But Blaettermann could not get along with his fellow faculty, his students, or his wife. Mrs. Blaettermann was no more popular than he; Jefferson's granddaughter Cornelia Randolph called her "a vulgar virago."

In 1835 Blaettermann outraged the faculty by painting the brick front of Pavilion IV. A century and a half later, one still sees faded red paint and clear penciling on its brick. It is almost certain that the penciling throughout the Lawn and

Range buildings was done to tone down Blattermann's defacement of Pavilion IV and to restore uniformity among the buildings. After fifteen years of almost constant dissension, he was finally dismissed in 1840 for twice cowhiding his wife—once publicly. He moved to the country and died of a stroke in 1842.

His successor was a Hungarian, Charles Kraitsir, who had participated in a Polish revolt against Russia. Domestic strife soon reoccurred in Pavilion IV, only in reverse: Mrs. Kraitsir began beating her husband and turning him out of the house at night. To restore peace on the Lawn, Kraitsir was dismissed in 1844.

Maxmilian Schele de Vere followed that year. A Swede by birth, a Prussian by allegiance, and a Frenchman by heritage—his father had gone from France to Sweden with Bernadotte—Schele de Vere received his professorship through Longfellow the poet. For fifty-one years, this elegant cosmopolite in his top hat set the styles on the Lawn.

In 1904 Edwin A. Alderman became the university's first president and set up his office here, as did the second president, John Lloyd Newcomb. In 1950 the third president, Colgate W. Darden, Jr., moved the president's office to Pavilion VIII.

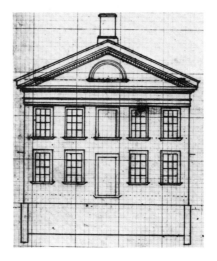

PAVILION VI

It is at once evident that although Pavilion VI is pedimented, instead of a two-story portico it has only the simple one-story Tuscan columns of the colonnade.

There are two types of one-story columns on the Lawn: the milk-bottle shape resulting from inferior work and the true Tuscan built to Jefferson's specifications. The latter rise in parallel straight lines, tapering slightly toward the top. The six columns fronting Pavilion VI adhere to the correct design and are set forward in the manner of other pavilions' two-story columns. These columns support Jefferson's elevated terrace walkway across the front of Pavilion VI. There are steps at both ends of it, and midway in the six student rooms between Pavilions VI and VIII there are brick steps leading down to Green Alley between the gardens of these pavilions.

In his description of his classic intent for the facade of Pavilion VI, Jefferson prescribed "the Ionic of the Theatre of Marcellus from Chambray." Since there are no two-story columns, this order was used for the pavilion's entablature. For the building's only ornamentation, both the entablature and the pediment are lined with strong dentils resting on a

smaller egg-and-dart molding, reversing the arrangement on Pavilion II. The pediment and lower-door transom contain fanlights of different designs.

Without a two-story portico, this sturdy, handsome house still conveys a sense of dignity. Two double-hung sash windows flank both upper and lower double doors. All the front windows have louvered blinds. Although all pavilions still retain some of their handmade holdbacks, only Pavilion VI, like Pavilion II, has all of its original ten.

After advertising in 1819 in northern newspapers, Jefferson accepted the bid of Richard Ware of Philadelphia to bring his own brickmakers and bricklayers to the university site. Ware's work was considered superior, and he is credited with building Pavilions II, IV, and VI. Except for plastering, Pavilion VI was finished in October 1822.

The first occupant of Pavilion VI was twenty-eight-year-old Charles Bonnycastle, a bachelor, who arrived from England in February 1825. He had been educated at the Royal Military Academy, Woolwich, where his father was professor of mathematics. He first taught natural philosophy, using the latest methods of instruction, but in 1827 transferred to mathematics. So shy he would climb a fence and walk in mud to avoid a student, he still soon managed to marry a red-

haired beauty, Ann Mason Tutt of Loudoun County. They had three children, and Bonnycastle relieved the generally bleak appearance of the pavilion gardens by adding a rose and honeysuckle arbor behind Pavilion VI under which they could play.

Bonnycastle was considered "amiable, gentleman-like and charming" and so knowledgeable that he could fill any chair. He was chairman of the faculty from 1833 to 1835. When he died at forty-four in 1840, his death was deeply lamented. He was buried in the university cemetery.

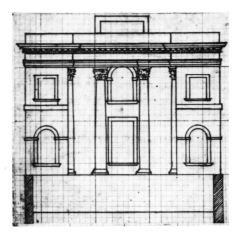

PAVILION VIII

In the stretch between Pavilions VI and VIII that is long enough to contain seven student rooms, Jefferson also included an opening to stairs leading down to Key Alley between the gardens of these pavilions. The facade of Pavilion VIII is unique because his design for it incorporated the recessed entrance of an Italian loggia. Pavilions VIII and IX, the two utilizing suggestions by Latrobe, are the only two with the recessed, or in antis, entrances. Here the classical motif is the Corinthian of the Emperor Diocletian's Baths, as taken from Chambray. On the specifications for this pavilion in his notebook, Jefferson wrote "Latrobe's Lodge front"; it is the only one of the pavilions on the East Lawn that he attributed to Latrobe.

Of Pavilion VIII's four two-story Corinthian columns, brick covered in white plaster, the two end ones are half-columns engaging the wall. Although the colonnade continues in front of this pavilion as it does at Pavilion VI, only a catwalk leads from its roof to the upstairs door. The tall columns behind the colonnade are freestanding so that light falls onto the entranceway. With this arrangement, Jefferson gave depth and complexity to Pavilion VIII. The elaborate Corinthian marble capitals were carved in Italy, and the en-

tablature is also Corinthian. The concrete bases were made locally. The parapet that once concealed Pavilion VIII's original semi-flat rooflets was long ago removed when the building was given a hipped roof to correct leakage.

Another strikingly individual feature of this facade is a pair of small projecting bays, whose walls create the recess of the entryway. On the lower floor, each bay contains an arched window, and two additional arched windows flank the doorway.

Upstairs, the center double doorway stands between two small double-sash windows without arches. All windows have louvered blinds, the first on the Lawn to be changed from bottle-green to the gray-brown color indicated by detailed study to have been the original color. At the same time, in 1986, the doors of Pavilion VIII were returned to their original wood-grain finish. The rather elaborate cornice of Pavilion VIII is lined with sharply carved modillions, under which is an egg-and-dart molding over dentils. William Coffee of New York executed the cornice.

The first occupants of Pavilion VIII were young Professor and Mrs. Thomas Hewett Key, who arrived in February 1825. Key had received degrees from Trinity College, Cambridge, and had studied medicine in London. His chair was mathematics, but he remained on the Lawn only two years before resigning to become professor of Latin at the University of London. He also became a founder of the London Library.

Following Key, a long roster of professors occupied Pavil-

ion VIII. One of them was fearless, red-haired mathematics professor William H. Echols, called "Reddy," whose fame as the hero of the Rotunda fire has endured even though his herculean effort to save the Rotunda by hurling dynamite from its roof into its flaming link with the Annex failed. The detonation was heard fifteen miles away. The bronze marker on Pavilion VIII commemorating his residency here says that "By precept and example, he taught many generations of students with ruthless insistence that the supreme values are self-respect, integrity of mind, contempt of fear and hatred of sham."

In the 1950s President Darden moved his office from the upstairs of Pavilion IV into Pavilion VIII, and it remained the president's office until 1984 when the office was moved to Madison Hall. Pavilion VIII was then converted into two faculty apartments with conference space on the main level, a return to the blend of living and learning intended by Jefferson for all pavilions.

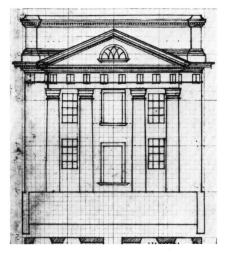

PAVILION X

Pavilion X is a four-columned, pedimented building of substantial dignity with well-scaled proportions. Along the colonnade from Pavilion VIII, there is access to Lile Alley behind and six steps descend where the Lawn makes its steepest drop. At the bottom one student room, No. 50, is wedged tightly against the pavilion's side. It gives the appearance of a small wing.

Ornamented in the Doric order of the Theater of Marcellus, as taken from Chambray's book, Pavilion X has the most

63

elaborate cornice of all the pavilions. The underside, or soffit, of the cornice in its Doric entablature contains rectangular blocks, each with eighteen guttae, or truncated cones. The blocks are separated by foliated ornaments of lead in diamond shapes containing a four-petaled rosette which some observers have likened to the dogwood blossom, Virginia's state flower. Each of the corner medallions contains an eight-petaled rosette that has been called a magnolia blossom. The entablature is topped with dentil molding. The Doric capitals were made locally.

Pavilion X has several features of design unique among the pavilions. Although he preferred columns standing on bases as the Romans built them, Jefferson drew Pavilion X's columns without them, in the Greek style espoused by his friend Latrobe. As built, these columns rest on square concrete bases, or plinths, that rise only about three inches above the colonnade's brick floor.

Pavilion X's gallery is only half the width of the other pavilions' galleries, but it is supported with tie-rods and has a trellis railing. The wooden parapet adapted from the Temple of Nerva Trajan that Jefferson gave Pavilion X was removed about 1870. Although he drew the same multiple arch for the pediment's lunette as that of Pavilion IV, this window has a conventional fanlight pattern. Jefferson's unfailing sense of balance made him place another student room, No. 52, on the pavilion's far side, giving the effect of a small matching wing.

The first tenant of this stately residence was Dr. Robley Dunglison, a Scot, aged twenty-six when he and his bride arrived with the Keys and Bonnycastle in February 1825. He had earned medical degrees in England and Germany and held a diploma from the Society of Apothecaries. He was already known as a writer on medical subjects.

Dr. Dunglison was the first full-time professor of medicine in an American university, and it was his decision that the university's medical diplomas be issued in English rather than in Latin. His contract was extraordinary then in that it restricted his practice outside the university to consultation.

He became first secretary of the faculty and its chairman in 1826 and chairman again in 1828–30.

Dunglison, as professor of medicine and anatomy, wanted an anatomical building in which to perform dissections. Jefferson, to fill this need, made a drawing before March 4, 1825, of an "Anatomical Theatre." He gave it a skylight over the operating area and lunetted windows above eye level for light without public gaze from outside. Dunglison must have been pleased when construction began before Jefferson died in 1826; the building was ready for use by February 1827. The only original university building ever to be demolished, it was torn down in 1938 to make room for Alderman Library.

In May 1825, when Jefferson's personal physician left Charlottesville, he commended his aged patient to Dunglison, who bought a horse and a slave to serve as its groom. Because the university stables had not been built, Dunglison may have stabled it in the village or built a shed for it in his garden. He attended Jefferson several times a week all summer, making a score of trips to Monticello. The more Jefferson saw of him, the better he liked him. At the beginning of Jefferson's last illness, when he was eighty-three, he summoned his trusted physician on June 24, 1826. The next week Dr. Dunglison returned to Monticello and stayed there, always on call. He was in the room on July 4, 1826, when the clock hands reached 12:50 P.M. It was he who told the family. Soon bells throughout the community began to toll.

Before the end of the nineteenth century, Pavilion X had been occupied in succession by four distinguished professors of law.

THE SOUTH END OF THE LAWN

On the grass before Pavilion X is the spot where the Lawn's only murder took place.

In the university's first summer, discipline among students became an immediate problem. Restless and rebellious

youths, many away from home for the first time, seemed inclined to take advantage of Jefferson's plan for their self-government. Many accustomed at home to drinking, gambling, and carrying firearms were unable to cope with their almost complete freedom at the university. Rowdyism struck the Lawn, and pistols and muskets were fired in the colonnades, with the sound of disorder reverberating into the pavilions. "Down with the European professors!" cried a group of masked students after dark in the early fall of 1825. From their West Lawn pavilions, professors Emmet and George Tucker came out to investigate; a brick was thrown at Emmet, and Tucker was attacked with a cane. Vulgar abuse was shouted at both. Certain professors threatened to resign.

Jefferson deplored these "vicious irregularities," and upon his recommendation the Visitors instituted extreme regulations: students must be in bed by 9:00 P.M., rise at dawn, breakfast by candlelight, and wear a dull gray uniform. No student could own a gun, a horse, or a dog. Smoking, gambling, and drinking were forbidden, and students were forced to deposit all funds with the proctor, who doled out small sums.

These rules were so deeply resented that in the 1830s three major riots occurred. Many pavilion windows were smashed, there was much firing of muskets under the arcades, and the door to Pavilion VI was battered in. Several professors were assaulted; the others armed themselves and retired to pavilion upper floors. In 1835 Professor Gessner Harrison, chairman of the faculty, was horsewhipped by two students while a hundred others watched the outrage.

The climax came on the night of November 12, 1840. When two masked students fired shots and caused an uproar on the Lawn, law professor John A. G. Davis, chairman of the faculty, came out of Pavilion X to investigate. It was 10:00 P.M. As Davis, near the north column of Pavilion X's portico, tried to remove one student's mask, the youth, Joseph E. Semmes of Georgia, drew a pistol and shot him fatally. Semmes was apprehended, released on $25,000 bail, and the case was carried to the Virginia court of appeals. He disappeared. One report said to Texas, another said to Georgia, and afterward he was believed to have committed suicide. The shock of Professor Davis's death brought students to their senses.

Under the guidance of Judge Henry St. George Tucker, Davis's successor in both the School of Law and Pavilion X,

the obnoxious rules were revoked. In the serious mood that followed this tragedy, the university's Honor System came into being in 1842.

To the south at the bottom of the Lawn are the buildings designed by Stanford White to replace the classroom space

lost when the Rotunda Annex burned. Because White planned to adhere to Jefferson's intention that the south end of the Lawn remain open, he proposed buildings on both sides of it but was overruled by the Board of Visitors. In the center stands Cabell Hall, formerly called the Academic Building. On the right is Cocke Hall, initially called the Mechanical Laboratory, and on the left Rouss Hall, once called the Physical Laboratory. All were built in 1896–98. Cabell Hall contains lecture rooms, offices, and a public hall seating 994. The University's second copy of Raphael's *School of Athens* is here. Cabell Hall was expanded greatly in 1952 with an addition on three sides that is known as New Cabell Hall.

On the right, a brick-paved boxwood niche holds a seated bronze of Jefferson by Karl Bitter. This statue was presented to the university by Charles R. Crane and unveiled on Founder's Day, April 13, 1915. It is said that this spot was chosen for the monument so that Jefferson might always see Monticello from the Lawn. Today, trees have cut off this view.

On the left, facing Jefferson from another leafy alcove, stands a majestic bronze of George Washington. It is a replica of Houdon's statue in the State Capitol in Richmond.

On the open grass in front of Cabell Hall, his sightless eyes toward the Rotunda, sits a bronze, forever patient, *Blind Homer with His Student Guide*. Representing all classical knowledge, this monument of the Greek poet was given to the university by John W. Simpson of New York City at the request of its sculptor, Moses Ezekiel, and was unveiled on June 10, 1907.

THE EAST
RANGE AND
GARDENS

Beyond the lower side of Pavilion X is a double flight of concrete stairs leading east to a walk along the periphery of Jefferson's original academical village. On the left, behind a stretch of serpentine wall on an elevation, is Pavilion X's double garden. Set into the wall is a reproduction of one of the original necessaries, or outhouses, on the grounds. All in the same pattern, these little garden houses were the height of elegance in their day, being built of brick with metal roofs, white louvers, and white doors. Only the necessaries in the outside garden walls were replaced to show the original appearance of the walled gardens. Here, above ground level, the four bricked-in trapdoors are plainly visible. Among this garden's trees, two paulownias overhang the little building and the garden wall. They reach the peak of their purple flowering in early May.

Jefferson did not invent serpentine walls. Almost surely he saw them in England in 1786, and he may have seen a type of them earlier at Governor Sir William Berkeley's Green Spring plantation, built about 1645 three miles west of Jamestown. But there can be no doubt that by placing such walls throughout the university's grounds, Jefferson brought them enduring appreciation.

Ahead, on the right, is the neo-Georgian Randall Hall, erected in 1899 by a private contribution from the estate of W. J. and Belinda Randall of Massachusetts. At first a student dormitory, it now houses the Department of History.

Immediately beyond Randall Hall stands the rectangular pre–Civil War brick addition to a pedimented brick building that Jefferson designed and called Hotel F. The older portion is obscured until one walks past the addition. A third mid-nineteenth-century building called the Crackerbox, a small brick cottage with a pitched roof, stands to the rear of Hotel F. These three units are all of two stories and constitute the southeast corner of Jefferson's academical village, at the south end of East Range. Although the front brickwork of the hotel is in Flemish bond, its rear and the other buildings are in variations of the common bond.

Jefferson chose to place six student refectories in the two outside rows of university buildings instead of one large mess hall in a central location. Each building was to be leased to an individual hotelkeeper, who would live in it with his family and feed no fewer than twenty-five students nor more than fifty in the basement refectory. By dispersing these dining facilities, Jefferson hoped to create an added opportunity for student study. Having profited from learning French at an early age, he wanted to lease the first hotel to a French family who would teach colloquial French at meals. And why not also hotels for teaching Italian, German, and Spanish? Unfortunately, competent foreign families were not available in rural Virginia, but other applicants soon appeared. Their interest in the hotels was based solely on the hope of financial gain and of educating their growing sons.

Although all the hotels were finished in 1822, they, like the pavilions, remained unoccupied until shortly before the university opened on March 7, 1825. By late 1824, John Gray, Jr., was living with his family in Hotel E, West Range. The first professor, George Long, who arrived from England in December 1824, took his meals with Gray.

The Visitors decided on October 7, 1826, that allowing the students to choose their quarters was not working; thenceforth, the proctor would assign each student to a hotel and room. In the same meeting the Visitors resolved that "the hotel-keeper shall furnish the students not only with diet, but with bedding and furniture ... fuel, candles and washing," and servants, all regulated by the faculty. Later the word "furniture" was carefully defined to include one bed per occupant, a table, two chairs, a looking glass, a washstand,

bowl, and water pitcher, and andirons. In 1842 written instructions specified that the hotelkeeper also was to supply a pair of tongs and a shovel, a candlestick, a pair of snuffers, and one clean towel daily per student. Duties and hours for servants were carefully spelled out.

Hotelkeepers were to prohibit gambling and the presence of "ardent spirits or wine mixed or unmixed." It was their further duty, once the bell rang at daylight, to assure that each janitor actually roused his students at 6:00 A.M. To do all this, hotelkeepers hired and supervised "help," the average per hotel being five, whom each paid unless he owned them. Servants built fires before dawn, exchanged ashes for firewood, brought shaving water (which sometimes froze on the way), polished mud-caked boots, and, while students were in class, made beds, swept dried clay from floors, "damp-wiped paint work," and "scoured" rooms.

The problems of the hotelkeepers began almost before they assumed their posts. The most basic was a lack of enough students to make the hotels pay. When the university opened, only thirty-three students were present. Two weeks later Jefferson wrote Madison that between fifty and sixty students were on hand and more were expected. When the session ended on December 15, 1825, there were 123 students. Only once in the university's first five years—in 1826 when there were 177 students on the grounds—were there enough students to support the six hotels.

For each student his hotel was not only his dining hall but a place of assembly, his club, his fraternity. This was especially true in the university's first two years, before the Rotunda was finished. Though student rebelliousness caused some disorder in hotels, a seriously disturbing factor was the behavior of the hotelkeepers themselves.

One week after the university opened, the proctor listed the hotelkeepers: Edwin Conway, Hotel A; S. B. Chapman, Hotel B; Warner W. Minor, C; George Washington Spotswood, D; John Gray, Jr., E; and James Byers, F. Four months later, Byers dropped out and was succeeded by J. B. Richeson.

By the following March, Richeson and Chapman had traded hotels. With the exception of Minor, these men were unable to resist drinking and gambling with students. Students, quickly finding Minor unwilling to play loo or whist, to drink wine, juleps, or toddies, or to lend them even small sums, branded him "close." He became so unpopular that by 1828 at least nine students declined to matriculate because they would have been assigned to his hotel.

As the Visitors and faculty struggled with the students and hotelkeepers to maintain a proper university environment, enrollment dropped to 128 in 1827, 131 in 1828, and 120 in 1829. Throughout all this, three meals per day were required on hotel tables. The hotelkeepers soon learned that the vegetable gardens behind the hotels were far from sufficient, and a sizable plot within the university precincts was reserved for each hotel on the border of the grounds, to the east of East Range. Later more gardening land farther off to the south and west was made available for those who would work the clay soil and cope with the summer droughts.

Meat and dairy products still had to be bought. This required a horse and some kind of wagon, rig, or hack in which to forage town and countryside. And cash, with which to pay. Adding thirty students to Spotswood's family of ten and five servants, one realizes he had forty-five people to feed continuously. Of all the hotelkeepers, Spotswood was the most tempestuous.

The rectangular brick addition to Jefferson's Hotel F was built in 1857 to serve as the university's first actual gymnasium. The white-painted bricks in its cornice are placed to resemble modillions in the neoclassical manner of the time. After Jefferson's exercise areas at the Rotunda became inadequate, students exercised in the open. In 1852 J. E. d'Alfonce, a genial, roly-poly Pole who became a French citizen and had been an officer in the Russian army, was authorized to teach gymnastics out of doors and to set up parallel bars beyond the south end of the Lawn.

D'Alfonce put the students, "all in an easy uniform of blue blouse and grey trousers," through "a series of complex exercises, marching and counter marching." Once the gym, Levering Hall, was erected, exercise, exclusive of the marching, was taken indoors. Within the gym, the students began "turning upon bars, swinging upon ropes, brandishing broadswords or foils, dumbbells or clubs." In 1876 Edward R. Squibb of New York gave funds to equip the gym with the most modern apparatus. Anna Barringer, who lived in Hotel F as a child in the 1890s, later recalled that the gymnasium "resounded at all hours with the thumping sound of men working out with dumbbells or Indian clubs. It was not a quiet corner."

Walking to the right around Levering Hall, the visitor reaches the south end of the arcaded East Range. Here stands Hotel F, the only two-story, pedimented hotel in the Ranges. Behind its one-story arcaded portico, three steps lead up to the hotel's double front doors, over which is a fanlight in the transom. The arcade provides an upper deck onto which double doors open. There are no railings here, and Jefferson's drawing of Hotel F shows none.

As a partial antidote to the early student rebelliousness that had distressed Jefferson, there began in 1828 a series of student balls that greatly improved relations among the various hotels and their assigned students. One notable ball was given in Hotel F on November 13, 1830. From the late 1820s into the 1840s, not a year passed without a ball given by the boarders of each active hotel. Generally, these were held in

Hotel C, the middle building of West Range, or, after 1831, in Hotel D on East Range. Later came the balls for the entire student body in the Dome Room of the Rotunda.

By 1834 fencing, dancing, and gymnastics were at the height of popularity at the university. Students made their own financial arrangements with instructors. Fencing and dancing classes had been held for several years in Hotels C and D, and in 1834 another teacher arrived, Corsican-born Major Alexander A. Penci, who became an instructor in fencing and gymnastics. He was given an upstairs room in Hotel F as a domicile and taught in Hotel C. In 1835 his family occupied the remainder of the upstairs of Hotel F. Penci became ill and, seeking warmer winters, moved to Havana, where he died about 1838.

Hotel F stands on a low bluff facing a grassy lawn bordered with large English box. Stretching away below is the university's Medical Center complex. In the early years this area was a serene, broad meadow, where the various hotels had their major vegetable plots and some fruit trees. Bordering the West Range was a similar area where the university stables were erected.

Abutting Hotel F on its north side is an upper room that was added over the adjoining student room. When Dr. Paul B. Barringer, professor of physiology and surgery, and his family occupied Hotel F in 1890, this became their third bedroom. The student room below was allotted them as a small sitting room, and two adjacent student rooms became Dr. Barringer's office. The Crackerbox behind served as the Barringer kitchen, with their cook's room upstairs.

Passing around to the rear of Hotel F, the visitor sees that the Crackerbox's enormous chimney is almost obscured by a large common boxwood. This little brick cottage, remodeled in 1967, has narrow rakeboards and an outside stair. It is considered a Range residence and houses two students upstairs and two below. Like other students on the Lawn and Ranges, they go out of doors and down to bath facilities.

The Barringer family also was allotted and cultivated the lower garden behind Pavilion X, then laid out in four ascending terraces. Vegetables and berries were grown, and there was a grape arbor across the lowest terrace. Shrubs and bulbs grew in corners and against the walls. Anna Barringer remembered that "there were no box bushes. There was a rumor that Mr. Jefferson never liked box, and there was none at Monticello."

THE PAVILION GARDENS

The tour of the East Lawn gardens begins with the garden of Pavilion X. Eight sandstone steps lead up to a white wooden gate in the wall at the bottom of Pavilion X's garden.

Although Jefferson was an avid gardener, he disliked the cold rigidity of formal, highly stylized French gardens such as those at Versailles. He liked the informal *jardin anglais*, which the French popularized. About the Lawn gardens, Fiske Kimball wrote in 1916 that Jefferson had adopted the French idea of a *cour d'honneur*, an upper pleasure garden, and a *cour de service*, a lower kitchen garden.

As laid out by Jefferson and as shown in the Maverick Plan of 1822–25, there are sixteen gardens behind the ten pavilions and the six hotels. The six pavilions having hotels behind them—three on East Lawn and three on West Lawn—originally shared their gardens with the six hotels. Both the East and West Lawn garden walls were first built in 1821–24, as a part of Jefferson's architectural plan for the university. He died before the gardens were entirely laid out, and he left no specific plan or design for their planting.

All the gardens are bordered on their sides by brick serpentine walls, and the shared gardens are divided approximately in their centers by serpentine walls. The bottom walls of all the gardens are straight brick walls, and on East Range, due to the terrain's sharp fall, these outer walls stand on heavy stone bases. For durability, all walls are brick capped. Also because of the terrain, the East Lawn pavilions reveal three stories in the rear.

Although pavilion families at times relax on their front galleries, from early days their tree-shaded pleasure gardens have contained some sort of small porch, long veranda, terrace, brick-paved sitting area, or parterre directly behind each house.

In the university's earlier days, when many families were large and servants performed household functions, the pavilion gardens, then often called "backyards," teemed. The horse-drawn carts and wagons of deliverymen crowded into the service lanes, now called "alleys," which Jefferson labeled "streets." The alleys, macadamized in 1826, were among the first streets so surfaced in America. Although it was not Jefferson's intention that the Lawn gardens should contain small dependencies other than the necessaries, the need arose early for woodsheds, washhouses, chicken coops, smoke or meat houses, and outbuildings for servants. On July 22, 1828, the Visitors authorized Dr. Dunglison and Dr. Emmet each to build servants' quarters costing no more than $150. Cows and hogs were not maintained in the vicinity of the Lawn. There were wells and cisterns, and later hydrants. Laundry was sometimes done out of doors and dried here. Nearly everyone grew vegetables and berries, and there were fruit trees. The accepted quota of servants was a cook, a housemaid, a nursemaid, and, when needed, a gardener.

In restoring the original walls, Maverick's engraving of Jefferson's plan was carefully followed for all architectural details such as the locations of replaced or repaired walls, walks, gates, steps, and even benches. The West Lawn gardens were restored in 1948–52 and the East Lawn gardens in 1960–65 by the Garden Club of Virginia. As Jefferson left no plans for their interior layouts and plantings, these are not restorations. The genius behind these designs was Alden Hopkins, a landscape architect who interpreted Jeffersonian ideals with such subtlety that the gardens give the impression of having existed since Jefferson's time. Although no gardens are closed to the public, the upper gardens adjacent to the pavilions are used by the pavilion families. A simple rule is, where gates are not marked "Private" and walks lead to openly placed benches, use them. Where gates are closed, they should be closed after one passes through; where open, they should be left open.

No two Lawn gardens are alike. They blend to form a continuous park through Jefferson's academical village. These green roofless rooms are leafy retreats, little coves of tranquillity, that offer something different in every season.

From the entrance to the lower garden behind Pavilion X, the ground rises sharply. A center gravel path leads up to a crosswalk below the dividing serpentine wall. Immediately inside the gate are two feathery American smoke trees.

In this garden all evidences of utilitarian gardening are long gone, and four gigantic clumps of common boxwood dominate. Between the box on each side of the walk stands a large Kentucky coffee tree. Although these trees did not originate in Kentucky, they are native to the Appalachian area, and although they do not bear coffee, they produce a similar-looking bean. Against their trunks are rounded metal benches.

At the crosswalk, below a steep bank planted with large-leaf periwinkle and yucca at random, steps on the left ascend to the necessaries. Overhanging them are the empress paulownias whose wood is unusually valuable because it is light in weight, strong, and so stable that it neither swells nor shrinks. The species was named in honor of the Grand Duchess Anna Paulovna, daughter of Czar Paul I of Russia.

To the right at the top of the stairs to the upper garden is a large hackberry tree. Under it, a white gate in one of Jefferson's many Chinese trellis patterns leads into the garden over the sanded foundation, outlined in brick, of a former necessary. A red mulberry shades this corner of the upper garden.

From the 1870s brick addition to Pavilion X, at that time the largest addition to any pavilion, double green wooden

stairs descend to the brick-paved family sitting area behind the house. In this garden the landscaping is curvilinear, supporting Jefferson's admiration for William Hogarth's use of the serpentine line as "the line of grace." This garden is the Lawn's widest. It has an elliptical grass plot cut by a curving brick walk and is dominated by four huge American holly trees. Evergreens form a backdrop against the three serpentine brick walls, with mountain laurel under two large saucer magnolias against the dividing serpentine wall. There are also willow, maple, and oak trees. Perennials are crocus, lily of the valley, Jeffersonia, daffodils, jonquils, daylilies, hyacinths, tansy, and Guernsey lilies. Autumn visitors are invariably pleased with the vivid chrysanthemums in this garden.

THE GARDEN OF PAVILION VIII

A solid-panel white gate in Pavilion X's upper garden leads to Lile Alley, named for William Minor Lile, who became professor of law in 1893 and was the fifth occupant of Pavilion X. Across the alley another solid gate opens onto another outhouse foundation midway in the garden of Pavilion VIII. This garden is laid out in four flowing tiers and has no center partition. For years this pavilion served as the university president's office, and the hourglass composition of the garden not only facilitated entertaining but also permitted outdoor conferences.

Tall crape myrtles on the left, against the serpentine wall, cast a vivid splash of midsummer color. A row of golden raintrees shades the center bank. Unsure that raintrees would survive Virginia winters, Jefferson nevertheless imported them from France. These were placed here to honor him. Under them are random clumps of yucca.

Pavilion VIII's three back stories are faced with a deep, unroofed gallery, supported by a triple-arch arcade. A white Chinese trellis railing tops the arcade, and its center arch is faced with clipped ivy. At the edge of a brick terrace in front of the arcade, the broad grassy ramp begins its sweep downward. Brick-bordered gravel walks flare out to enclose the top grassy level. These are flanked by dogwoods and below them by red maples of various sizes. Fanning out to the side walls are box, summer perennials such as oakleaf hydrangea and bottlebrush buckeye, and beds of spring bulbs.

Below the ramp, on the third level, the walks converge above a wide, brick staircase. There are tiger lilies about.

The stairs lead down into a small decorative orchard on the lowest level. It stands in a rectangle of gravel walks that enclose common apple and Seckel pear trees planted in a semiformal parterre of diagonals, bordered on its three outer sides by beds of periwinkle. At the center of the bottom boundary wall, a white Chippendale garden bench stands out against the dark green of southern magnolias. These are flanked by pecan trees and two English walnuts. In the southeast corner is a black walnut. Two sour cherry trees, one still bearing, stand against the northeast serpentine wall bordering Key Alley, named for Thomas Hewett Key, first professor of mathematics and Pavilion VIII's first occupant. On the top terrace, a gate to the right leads into Key Alley.

HOTEL D

At the bottom of Key Alley, a lane passes behind Hotel D on the left, the center building in the East Range. The metal hipped roof of this one-story brick lodge terminates in a large, square center chimney. Harmonizing with the Lawn's usual architectural motifs, Hotel D has a fanlight in both its front and rear door transoms, and an arcade fronts it.

Hotel D has served many purposes. For several years it was one of Jefferson's six original dining halls, but when enrollment did not support all the hotels, Arthur S. Brockenbrough, the proctor, moved with his family into it. As an experienced builder, Brockenbrough from 1819 on had relieved Jefferson greatly by overseeing construction. In 1831 Hotel D was alloted to a Monsieur Ferron for what he called his "fencing academy." Terming himself a "maître d'armes,"

he gave instructions in fencing, singlestick, and boxing. Soon he was also teaching dancing.

When student balls came into fashion, Hotel D was a favorite place for giving them. Later it became the center for alumni activities and in the late nineteenth century was

called Alumni Hall. It and the university post office next
door in Room 22 brought much traffic to East Range. When
a new and far larger Alumni Hall was needed in the twentieth
century, Hotel D once again became a residence, for faculty
or official university guests.

THE GARDEN OF PAVILION VI

The garden of Pavilion VI is up three steps and through a white gate in the long brick wall behind Hotel D.

Inside, four brick steps lead under a pair of maple trees into the lowest tier of Pavilion VI's three-tiered garden. Once the vegetable garden for Hotel D, this area has been given the eighteenth-century seminaturalistic treatment of an English country garden. Trees native to Virginia—white pines, Norway spruces, maples, and a sour gum—were planted around the four walls to create background woodland thickets. Against these are set visitor benches. This is the only Lawn garden intentionally planned as a wilderness garden.

In the garden's open center, ringed with a sanded path, is a sandstone Gothic pinnacle dating from 1451, presented to the university in 1927 by Merton College of Oxford. A weaving path cushioned with pine needles leads to the garden's inner right-hand corner, up curving steps bordered with yuccas and ferns. At the top the two-tiered, tree-shaded upper garden is entered through a gate in the undulating wall.

A row of white pines on the lower side of the serpentine

division completely cuts off the lower, rustic garden. Set in the pines are two large red oaks that add to the screen. In the upper garden, a huge feathery mimosa overhangs the south end of the terrace and its benches, spreading its filtered shade over a small center grove of greengage plums. There are squared gravel walks under the plums. A fine English box hedge crosses the garden to cut off this level.

At each end of the box hedge, narrow brick steps lead up to a grass terrace with benches. From it, center brick steps lead to the pavilion family's sitting terrace. In May one of the brightest spots in all the Lawn gardens is the brief but flaming yellow of a single laburnum tree in this upper garden. Through the gate at the corner of the upper garden is Green Alley, named for Dr. Bennett W. Green, a physician, one of the founders of the Colonnade Club, and a benefactor of the university library in the early twentieth century. In the parking area between Pavilions VI and IV are two large chinaberry trees.

THE GARDEN OF PAVILION IV

Entering the single garden of Pavilion IV on the center of its three terraces, the visitor finds a grass plot bordered by flowering peach and cherry trees and sees lush English box on both sides. The first boxwood on the Lawn was planted in this garden by Professor Schele de Vere, who taught modern languages at the university from 1844 to 1895. His box, which no longer survive, were set in a small parterre below the brick sitting terrace for the enjoyment of his invalid wife, born Lucy Brown Rives of Castle Hill in Albemarle County.

Because Pavilion IV is not centered in its grounds, its garden gains a unique and pleasing imbalance. From the middle terrace, broad brick steps set in large English box lead up to a circular brick walk on the top level. This encloses a round island of huge English box, the finest on the Lawn. Southern magnolias provide shade for this level, and under them are portable backless benches. Beyond, the pavilion's brick terrace is reached from the house by double wooden stairs bordered with a Chinese trellis railing. There is no addition to Pavilion IV.

From the center terrace, brick steps lead down to a lower grassy lawn ringed with a circular walk bordered in brick. The south side of this lower garden is dominated by a large black locust tree. Under it stands a square cast-iron Corinthian capital which once capped a north portico column of the Rotunda Annex and survived the 1895 fire.

On the north side of this level, a scarlet oak in one corner and a northern catalpa in the other offset the locust. In June the catalpa is rich with small, lavender-touched blooms. Perennials near it are the blue-flowered spiderwort and a large sweetshrub, which produces brown flowers in early summer. Against the straight bottom wall, a long hedge of English box is interrupted by a white Chippendale bench. From it can be observed the arched muntins in the pavilion pediment's half-moon window and the matching counterpart in the back door's transom. This is a pleasing spot in which to rest a bit, and one may even speculate upon where Professor Blaettermann's two smokehouses stood long ago. The fact that he built the extra one added to the faculty's irritation with him.

THE GARDEN OF PAVILION II

The north gate on Pavilion IV's center terrace leads to Rotunda Alley. Across the way is a gate to the garden of Pavilion II, on the center of three levels. On the left overhanging the alley are a large holly, a gingko, and a black walnut. Narrow brick steps climb up to the pavilion's private garden.

Ahead, a short center walk flanked with Seckel pear trees leads into a square outdoor sitting area. Pear trees overhang facing white benches against a backdrop of grapevines, small fig trees, and blueberries. Beyond, the walk resumes between more pears and then divides; one way leads to a garden toolhouse that was once a necessary against the academical village's northernmost serpentine wall. The other way climbs brick steps up to the private family garden.

These two levels are divided by a southern bayberry hedge set in large-leaf periwinkle. On the upper terrace a gigantic native hardshell pecan tree, which is still bearing, casts its lacy shade over the bank. In the center of the upper garden stands a large-leaf magnolia.

Like all pavilions on East Lawn, Pavilion II reveals three stories at its back. From its two-story brick addition with a small unroofed wooden porch, double wooden stairs bordered with a Chinese trellis railing lead down to a wide brick terrace. Under the porch is a ground-floor entrance.

Set in the dividing serpentine wall is a white lattice gate. It opens onto four steps into the lower garden, once the vegetable garden for Hotel B. The bank on the left is planted with the yellow-flowering ground cover known as St.-John's-wort. On the right is an elderberry bush. The center of this garden is a small plum orchard, of four different varieties, planted around two crabapples in four rectangular plots.

Flanking both ends of the rectangles, three common apple trees stand against the outer serpentine walls. Below the plum orchard, the falling terrain creates a bank that rolls down to the garden's bottom wall. In the center of the bank, brick steps lead down to a gate in the wall. Yellow daylilies border the garden stairs. These stairs and the gate lead to a walk behind Hotel B. To the left, down six steps and at the end of the walk, is a marker set in the outside of the garden wall. It commemorates the Garden Club of Virginia's planting of the East Gardens, "the creation of three landscape architects: Alden Hopkins, Donald Howard Parker, and Ralph Esty Griswold."

HOTEL B

The building across the way at the north end of East Range is Hotel B. Its north entrance has a small Doric portico with two white columns and a pedimented roof. Not shown on the Maverick Plan, this portico probably was added when the stone marked "The Washington Society 1869" was placed over the double doors. This student organization, called "The Wash," was formed in 1831; its formal name is the Washington Literary Society and Debating Union. It was in abeyance for two extended periods after 1929 but was revived in 1979 and today serves as a forum for debates and literary presentations to which the public is invited. The society meets on Thursdays at 7:30 P.M. in Pavilion VIII. Membership is open to all university students including graduate students.

Hotel B now houses university offices. The building has a side entrance under the East Range arcade.

One returns to the Lawn to continue the tour. The most direct route is up the brick walk outside the serpentine wall of Pavilion II's garden. On the left at the Rotunda, seven concrete steps lead up to the portico of Pavilion II. Directly across the Lawn is Pavilion I.

WEST LAWN

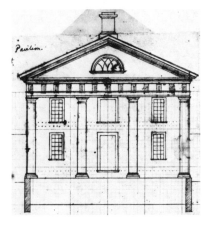

PAVILION I

Jefferson chose the Doric order of Diocletian's Baths in Rome from Chambray's book for the exterior of Pavilion I. With the columns of Pavilion II in the Ionic and the Rotunda's columns in the Corinthian order, the Doric on Pavilion I brought the three great classic orders within a few feet of each other at the top of the Lawn. Thus, a single turn of the head still introduces a student to the greatness of classical architecture, as Jefferson planned. It was also appropriate for Jefferson the farmer to use in rural Virginia the Doric with

the head of Saturn, the Roman god of agriculture, in the metopes between the triglyphs of Pavilion I's frieze. These ornaments were modeled and cast by William Coffee of New York.

Pavilion I was begun in 1819, finished in 1822, and was the fifth pavilion to be built. With its two-story, pedimented, four-column portico the same width as the house, it forms the central block of a typical Palladian building, but without flanking elements. Its plastered white-painted Doric columns rest on conventional Roman bases of concrete and wear painted concrete capitals in the Doric form, which were made in Charlottesville. The columns provide variety on the Lawn by being farther apart than any of the other classical examples Jefferson chose for portico columns. The building has a semicircular lunette in its tympanum and a square center chimney.

The upper gallery, like those of other pavilions, is supported by iron tie-rods suspended downward behind the columns. The gallery is approximately one foot narrower than the "raised terrace" that roofs the colonnade southward past all the original buildings on West Lawn. The gallery's white wooden railings are in one of Jefferson's many varying Chinese trellis designs. The portico above has a wooden ceiling, and the gallery floor provides a similar ceiling for the area below.

The house has center doorways upstairs and down. Both doorways are flanked by a double-sash window on each side. On the lower left, visible behind the old glass, is the pavilion's stairway angling upward. Outside, the offset in the hand-tooled brickwork shows how the pavilion and student room No. 1 were fitted together.

The first occupant of Pavilion I was Dublin-born Dr. John Patton Emmet, a nephew of the Irish patriot, who had been brought to America at the age of eight. He became a citizen and was one of the eight original professors. He was a bachelor of twenty-nine when he arrived on the Lawn from South Carolina to teach natural history and chemistry. Incredibly

versatile, he had an inventive mind that must have pleased Jefferson, on whom he called almost at once. Soon he wrote his father, "I have dined several times in the family. . . . [Jefferson is] an extremely pleasant old man and as hospitable as can be. We all take the greatest delight in promoting his views."

An early visitor to the Lawn observed that Dr. Emmet was "charming in manner and interesting in conversation." Fastidious, he complained to the proctor about the condition of his pavilion and lost no time submitting a plan for the addition of another room for lectures and laboratory. Jefferson noted on the back of this, "rec'd 12 May 1825."

Emmet had attended West Point and taught mathematics there. For his health he then spent a year in Naples, where he studied Italian, music, sculpture, and painting, and he next earned an M.D. in New York. He suggested that a vacuum of air could generate propulsive power, believed that chemistry could force the growth of vegetables, and was so interested in botany that it was inevitable Jefferson should call upon him, along with Abbé Correa de Serra, to help plan the university's proposed botanical garden.

Emmet was surprised when Jefferson assigned him to teach zoology, geology, and mineralogy in addition to natural history and chemistry, and when Jefferson added botany, he was appalled. Although Jefferson's death relieved Emmet of the botany classes, he bought land in the country just beyond the university precincts, named it Morea, and plunged deeply into plant experimentation. He set out Chinese mulberry trees to experiment with silkworms and manufactured his own vegetable and mineral dyes. He grew European grapes for wines and brandies, coffee trees, pyracantha hedges for fences, rare fruit trees, new esculents such as the eggplant, and flowers unknown in Virginia. He even tested edible acids, seeking the best method of curing Virginia hams. Emmet also experimented at length with steam for the generation of rotary motion. He composed sonnets, drew quick impressionist sketches, chiefly comic, and proved that Virginia kaolin clay was a good material for pottery and porcelain vases. Not long after his arrival, Emmet brought to live with him in Pavilion I a white owl, a brown bear, trays of silkworms, and numerous snakes. Then Emmet married Mary Byrd Tucker, a niece of George Tucker, first professor of moral philosophy. Soon the snakes were eliminated, the owl was freed into the woods, the silkworms were moved to the country, and the Emmets gave a sumptuous dinner in their cleaned and polished pavilion. The main course was a multi-seasoned bearmeat ragout. In 1834 the Emmets built a house on the Morea land and moved there from Pavilion I.

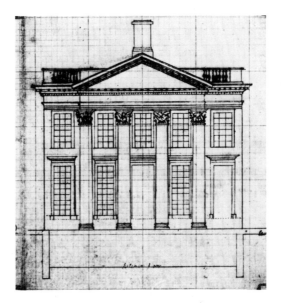

PAVILION III

Pavilion III was the most expensive pavilion to build; originally the largest of the pavilions, it is now the smallest. It derives distinction from the elegance of its classical details. The Corinthian capitals of its two-story portico, like those of the Rotunda, are of Carrara marble. As much as Jefferson wanted to use local stone for all capitals, the Italian masons he brought over found it unsuitable for the Corinthian or-

der; it did not carve properly, and some of it did not resist weathering. These capitals, with their delicate, detailed acanthus leaves, had to be carved in Italy.

Finally, delivered to the Lawn by oxcart from tiny Milton on the Rivanna River where they had arrived by bateaux, they were considered highly extravagant by everyone except Jefferson. To save the Virginia taxpayer customs duty, Jefferson declared them "educational materials" to be used in teaching architecture. The hand-carved wooden modillions in the soffit and pediment of Pavilion III repeat the acanthus leaf and are the finest on the Lawn. They rest on egg-and-dart molding over dentils. Jefferson labeled the classical motif of this building "the Corinthian of Palladio," as shown in Leoni's edition of the Italian architect's works.

To create variety and to accentuate its diminutiveness, Jefferson gave Pavilion III a two-story portico narrower than the house. Because its columns are closer together than those of the other pavilions on West Lawn, less of the trellis railing of the gallery is visible between the columns. Originally, the house had two front entrances. The center one led directly into the classroom. The side door, opening into a narrow hall, remains the family entrance. Its transom repeats the fanlight of the pediment, although Jefferson's drawing shows neither transom nor pediment window. Because two of the five bays are doorways, there are only three triple-sash, or walk-out, windows. On both sides of Pavilion III, offsets in the brickwork indicate how the building was set between the abutting student rooms. The house has the usual single center chimney and until after 1870 retained its parapet, which accentuated its cubistic form. The portico has a wooden ceiling, and beneath the gallery, its floorboards form another ceiling.

Though Pavilion III was one of those finished by September 30, 1821, it was empty when the university opened three

and a half years later and was the last pavilion to be occupied. From the start Jefferson wanted it to become the School of Law, but Francis Walker Gilmer, his choice for the chair, was delayed while recruiting professors in Europe and died soon after his return to Virginia, before he could take the position. After many frustrations, Madison nominated John Tayloe Lomax of Fredericksburg.

Born at Port Tobacco, Caroline County, Lomax graduated at age sixteen from St. John's College, Annapolis. The only native-born Virginian on the original faculty, he arrived a few days after Jefferson died. He occupied Pavilion III until 1830, when he resigned to become a judge of the circuit court. He was succeeded by Professor John A. G. Davis, who later moved to Pavilion X and there met his death at the hand of a student.

In addition to the Office of the Dean of the Graduate School of Arts and Sciences, for a quarter of a century in the 1900s Pavilion III also contained seminar rooms. In 1925 it became the birthplace of the *Virginia Quarterly Review*, a national journal of literature and discussion which Professor James Southall Wilson founded in the small inner room of the pavilion's basement. This room served as the *Review*'s office for three years until it was moved to Hotel A at One West Range.

South from Pavilion III along the colonnade, to the right at the first opening between the student rooms, is Poe Alley. Down five brick steps and a few feet out is a brick-bordered medallion honoring Poe, set into the paving. This flat disk, six feet in diameter, depicts the "stately Raven ... perched upon a bust of Pallas." The years 1809–1849 in the border tell Poe's life span, while the date 1826 commemorates his one session as a student at the university.

The two-story brick house attached to the back of Pavilion V, visible at the top of Poe Alley, is a faculty residence. This late-nineteenth-century addition has an entrance on the side with one-story white columns supporting a triple arch. It overlooks Pavilion V's garden, to which there is a Poe

Alley entrance. The house, entered by a brick walk between large English box, is referred to as "Pavilion V, Poe Alley." Pavilion V is the only Lawn residence with two separate units, sharing a common wall but without interior access between the two units.

At the top of Poe Alley on its north side, occupying ground cut off from Pavilion III's garden, is a small one-story brick building used as an administrative office. Dating only from the mid-twentieth century, it replaced another building on the same spot.

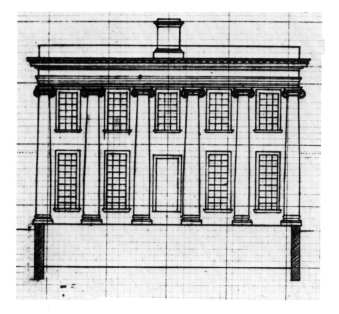

PAVILION V

Back on the Lawn, past three more student rooms, is Pavilion V. Its massive two-story, six-column portico is generally considered the most impressive of the pavilion facades. In his architectural notes Jefferson described its classical motif as "the Ionic of Palladio," found in the Leoni edition of 1721. Its six marble capitals were carved in Italy. There are dentils

and an egg-and-dart molding over the plain entablature, and rosettes are placed between the uncarved modillions.

Jefferson's drawing shows five bays on the upper floor without indicating that the center is a door leading out onto the gallery. Below, four triple-sash windows flank the center door. All have Chinese trellis railings and louvered blinds in bottle green. The gallery railing has three contrasting trellis patterns.

The first tenant of Pavilion V was George Long, professor of ancient languages. From Trinity College, Cambridge, and only twenty-four, Long moved into his new, unfurnished residence early in December 1824. Then the only resident on West Lawn, even in heavy snows he took his meals at Hotel E, West Range, which had been opened by John Gray, Jr., and was awaiting students.

Long acquired a black servant, sent to Richmond for furnishings, and soon called on Jefferson. He was received, he wrote many years later, by a "tall dignified old gentleman" who asked, "Are you the new Professor of Ancient Languages?"

"I am, sir."

"You are very young."

"I shall grow older, sir."

"That is true," Jefferson said, with a smile.

Long wrote, "I was pleased with his simple Virginia dress, and his conversation free from affectation." Other visits followed, Long dined at Monticello, and of him Jefferson wrote Cabell, "He appears to be a most amiable man, of fine understanding, well qualified for his department, and acquiring esteem as fast as he becomes known."

As soon as Long's books arrived by water, he began preparing his courses. Having known Professor and Mrs. Key in London he was congenial with them, and at the dining hall he met Harriet Selden, the attractive young widow of an

Arkansas judge who had been killed in a duel. She and Mrs. Gray were sisters of Arthur Brockenbrough, the proctor. During the university's first session, Long and Mrs. Selden fell so in love that a student-inspired couplet began circulating on the Lawn: "Harriet wants but little here below / But she wants that little Long!"

Despite his youthfulness, Long quickly established exacting standards in his school and stamped it with a contagious scholarship. His most brilliant pupil was Gessner Harrison. In 1828 when Long returned to England, taking his American wife, Harrison became professor of Latin and Greek at age twenty-two.

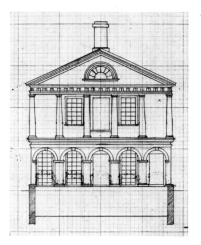

PAVILION VII

The next pavilion, Pavilion VII, is also called the Colonnade Club. In addition to being the oldest building on the Lawn, it is the only pavilion fronted with an upper one-story portico over an arcaded first floor. Its design bears a resemblance to what is presumed to be an early study for Monticello. Jefferson drew it in 1817, a year and a half before the General Assembly chartered the university. When the pavilion's cornerstone was laid on October 6 of that year, only its foun-

ON 6 OCTOBER 1817, IN THE
PRESENCE OF THOMAS JEFFERSON,
JAMES MADISON, JAMES MONROE,
AND MANY ANOTHER DISTINGUISHED
CITIZEN, WAS LAID THE CORNER-
STONE OF THIS PAVILION, THE FIRST
TO BE ERECTED OF THE GROUP THAT
WAS LATER TO GIVE VISIBLE FORM
TO JEFFERSON'S ARCHITECTURAL PLAN
FOR THE UNIVERSITY OF VIRGINIA

dation had been raised. The ceremony clearly signified, however, that his forty-year struggle to found "an University" was drawing to a close. A bronze plaque on the brick wall beside its doorway marks this event. Three presidents of the United States, Jefferson, Madison, and Monroe, as well as "the entire population of the town," were present.

Pavilion VII is midway between the Rotunda and Cabell Hall. On May 27, 1817, Jefferson received a sketch for a pavilion with an arcade supporting the Doric order from Dr. William Thornton, the architect of the U.S. Capitol in Washington. Jefferson described the classical motif he used here as the "Doric of Palladio" and took it from an illustration in Chambray. By placing a portico with six columns on a five-arched arcade carried by six sturdy, square plastered piers that make their return to the building's facade, Jefferson achieved a house of enormous solidity. The stabilizing pediment has the wide center mullion of the Rotunda arcade lunettes.

Here Jefferson introduced features he later used in the other pavilions: the deep gallery rather than a narrow balcony; the upper center door and its flanking windows; the

lower center door; the triple-sash windows of the classroom on the main floor, behind lattice railings; and the family entrance on the right.

Pavilion VII housed the university's first library, for which Jefferson at eighty-one in 1824 personally compiled the catalogue of 6,860 volumes. When the first boxes from Boston, London, and Paris arrived, William Wertenbaker placed them temporarily upstairs, but there were no shelves and the arrangement was inconvenient. The students read in the basement, and on cloudy days candles were sometimes needed. Upon completion of the Rotunda in September 1826, removal of the library to the Dome Room began. For years afterward Pavilion VII was known as "The Old Library."

Although the earliest faculty meetings were held in the various pavilions, as classes were moved into the Rotunda and pavilion classrooms passed to family use the faculty began to convene in Pavilion VII. Thus, in the days of student rebelliousness, culprits were called to faculty judgment here. Pavilion VII also became the center of religious activities at the university after 1832 when the faculty and students collaborated in raising funds to establish a chaplaincy. Chaplains were drawn from the clergy of Charlottesville, who upon faculty request had been holding services for students since 1828. They served for one-year terms until 1848 and for two years thereafter. Jefferson had anticipated services in one of the Rotunda rooms, and in 1841 one of its gymnasia wings was fitted out as a chapel. At least a part of Pavilion VII was set aside for the chaplain from 1843 until 1855 when a two-story parsonage was erected by public subscription on a small hill in the grounds southwest of the Lawn. From then until 1907, Pavilion VII was a faculty residence, although only three professors lived in it. In 1856 an expansion at the rear added four rooms, the present stair hall, and an additional basement. Gas for lighting was also installed then.

The next major event in the pavilion's history was the founding of the Colonnade Club by forty-two gentlemen on April 23, 1907, ten days after the 165th anniversary of Jefferson's birth. The club encourages social intercourse among faculty and alumni and promotes the interest and welfare of the university. The Visitors leased Pavilion VII to the club. Because of the club's close relationship with the university's General Alumni Association, "Alumni Annex" was added to Pavilion VII in 1913, extending the building far beyond its 1856 lines. Utilizing garden space, this addition provided the present large reading room, eight bedrooms with connecting baths, an even larger basement, storerooms, and a rear pergola overlooking the garden. Even though the new mortar joints were not scored in eighteenth-century tooling, the style of this annex is now called Colonial Revival.

Distinguished visitors entertained at the Colonnade Club include Lord Bryce, the British ambassador, and Lady Bryce; Count Carlo Sforza, once Italian foreign minister; President Harry S. Truman; and President Sukarno of the Indonesian Republic. In 1983 the club was given an extensive refurbishing.

In recognition of the 160th anniversary of Jefferson's design of Pavilion VII, a commemorative bronze plaque dated July 7, 1977, appeared quietly in the outside edge of the arcade's brick floor in front of the building's door. It was placed there by the Seven Society, whose members become known only after their death. From the time of its founding early in the twentieth century, the society has contributed liberally to many important university causes.

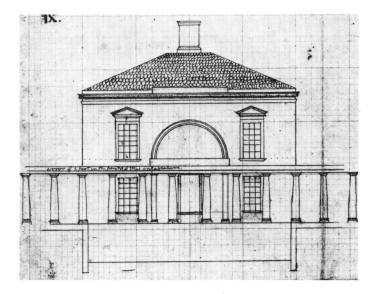

PAVILION IX

Down eight stone steps in the colonnade, a student room adjoins Pavilion IX on its north side, as does a similar room on the south; they create the effect of one-story wings, comparable to those across the Lawn that flank Pavilion X.

Pavilion IX brings a touch of French neoclassicism to the Lawn. Although Jefferson chose its Ionic motif from the Roman Temple of Fortuna Virilis, as shown in Palladio, it also reflects influence from Claude-Nicolas Ledoux's Hôtel de Guimard, built in 1770. Jefferson could have admired this elegant town house when in Paris, and his attention was almost surely redirected to it by Latrobe. With his deep interest in French neoclassical architecture, it was only natural that he should wish to incorporate some French reference into at least one pavilion. That Latrobe, whom he had asked for suggestions, contributed to the design of Pavilion IX, as well as that of Pavilion VIII, is borne out by the inscription of his name in Jefferson's hand on the drawing for this pavilion. Latrobean features could be the low hipped roofs and one-story flat-roof porticoes of both Pavilion VIII and IX. Pavilion IX has been called the most distinctive pavilion. With Pavilion III, it is now one of the two smallest.

Pavilion IX's difference in line and feel is immediately evident. The exedra form of its front entrance is its most significant feature. From a distance this stark white, plastered, half-domed doorway, recessed into weathered brick walls, is striking. Even the green double doors in the exedra are curved. The doorway is framed with two one-story Ionic columns and two Ionic pilasters in antis.

Because the house is intentionally dominated by its entrance, the front contains only four windows, all triple sash. The upper two permit access to the colonnade roof-terrace or gallery, while the lower windows have trellis rails. The building's only decorative molding is a single line of dentils, so fine as almost to be overlooked, in the plain entablature and in the exedra. Pavilion IX still has a slate roof in conformity with Jefferson's design.

The first resident of Pavilion IX was George Tucker, forty-year-old who soon became the most popular of the original professors. Born on Bermuda, Tucker came to the College of William and Mary at twenty to study law under his cousin St. George Tucker. In 1800 he joined the Richmond bar, and in 1802 he married Maria Carter, a great-niece of George Washington. He attained citizenship, settled in Lynchburg, and was elected to three terms in Congress. He wrote several books including a novel; one volume of essays prompted Madison to recommend him as professor of moral philosophy. Because he was the only Virginia resident of the faculty yet appointed, on April 12, 1825, he was elected first chairman of the faculty for a one-year term. As he did not arrive until a few days later, the only other American citizen on the faculty, Emmet, briefly served for him. Tucker was chairman twice again, in 1828 and 1832. Ever genial with keen humor, he was a superb raconteur. He held his post for twenty years, allowing Pavilion IX to be recognized as the School of Moral Philosophy. In 1845 he resigned and moved to Philadelphia in order to write. He died in 1861.

Tucker was succeeded in teaching moral philosophy by the Reverend William Holmes McGuffey, who became the second resident of Pavilion IX. A Presbyterian clergyman and educator, McGuffey was a vivid metaphysician and lecturer and the first cleric on the teaching staff. Born in Pennsylvania in 1800, he had been a professor at Miami University and Woodward College in Ohio and president of Cincinnati College and Ohio State University before coming to Virginia in 1845. McGuffey held national fame for his *Eclectic Readers*, the most popular language textbooks for American children ever published. Portraying children in constructive family roles, the *Readers* so widely influenced the nineteenth-century American mind that McGuffey was called "America's schoolmaster." He became one of the university's most celebrated teachers of the nineteenth century, and his presence tended to counteract a rather wide impression that the university was an "infidel institution."

McGuffey usually dressed in black, including old-fashioned knee breeches, and carried a cane, and his students dubbed him "Old Guff." Among the subjects he taught as professor of moral philosophy were ethics, logic, psychology, sociology, and political economy. In an age of flowery oratory, students welcomed his clear voice and simple language. To the surprise of many, his classes became so popular that students sometimes stamped their feet in approval. Once he stopped them with biting sarcasm: "Asses show their approval by their bray, their disapproval by their heels."

McGuffey was fervently religious. For two and one-half years he was the substitute minister in the Charlottesville Presbyterian Church, and he also preached in the local Methodist and Baptist churches. He held daily prayer meetings in Pavilion IX shortly after dawn that were voluntarily well attended by students and stimulated some into missionary work in the nearby mountains. McGuffey helped bring about the establishment at the university in 1857–58 of the first collegiate-affiliated YMCA in the United States. Together with his close friends General Cocke and law professor John B. Minor, he was a stalwart in the local temperance movement. He also crusaded for public schools. On a trip west he obtained funds to complete the payment for the construction of the university chaplain's residence.

Although the university continued classes throughout the Civil War, in 1864 enrollment fell to its lowest figure ever—fewer than fifty students, either wounded veterans or boys too young for military duty. Still McGuffey held his post, and in 1865 he went north, using his fame to solicit funds and to recruit students for the university. Old Guff's bite never lessened, and his popularity endured. Two years before he died in 1873, he finished a four-volume textbook on philosophy, of which one volume was published. He was buried in the university cemetery.

Beyond student room No. 55, past the West Lawn colonnade and an enormous hedge of common box, down seven steps and to the right, screened by more box at the lower

side of Pavilion IX, is a small one-story brick building known as McGuffey Cottage. It was erected after 1850 as a new kitchen for Pavilion IX. It is said that Professor McGuffey used it as his study. The cottage has a small shady garden with an entrance into Pavilion IX's garden. Like the Crackerbox on East Range, it is considered a grounds residence and is usually occupied by an unmarried professor. Towering above the box in front of the cottage still stands a large ancient black locust descended from the early black locusts that were the first trees authorized by the Visitors on the Lawn.

Ahead, toward the southwest end of West Range, over the serpentine wall on the right is the university's most magnificent tree. Standing on the far side of the garden of Pavilion IX, it is a Biltmore ash known as the McGuffey Ash. It is the largest ash tree in Virginia. According to Tucker family lore, this tree was planted by Professor Tucker shortly after his arrival in 1825. McGuffey legend ascribes his name to it because he convened children under it to test material for revised editions of his *Readers*. Both claims are very likely true.

THE WEST RANGE AND GARDENS

HOTEL E

Past the southwest corner of Pavilion IX's divided garden and at the south end of West Range is the student refectory Jefferson called Hotel E. This brick building has provided no student dining for many years, but during the academic year it now is open to faculty and administrative staff for lunch and special dinners. It is known as the Colonnade Hotel.

Of one story with a basement kitchen, it acquired a two-story annex soon after 1858 to provide more student dining space as the university grew. The addition in the simple early Victorian style is comparable to that of Hotel F and has the same white-painted brick cornice.

A brief detour to the front of Hotel E shows that the orig-

119

inal building is a squat structure with a slate hipped roof. It has two chimneys for fireplaces in reception rooms flanking a center hall. This hotel, like four of the others, is fronted with a three-arch arcade. Originally it had a parapet.

When genial John Gray, Jr., became the proprietor of Hotel E late in 1824, he had excellent prospects. His wife was a sister of the proctor, and their family was well known. That Gray had seven children to support did not deter him, however, from drinking and gambling with students. When he began ignoring faculty ordinances, Mrs. Gray fulfilled them as best she could, but after two years Gray was compelled to forfeit his lease. He departed for Florida, and Mrs. Gray simply stayed put, running the hotel properly. Although Mrs. Gray sought no sympathy, her sister Harriet Long, mistress

of Pavilion V, must have been a comfort until the Longs moved to England in 1828.

Soon one John Carter leased Hotel E and sublet it to Mrs. Gray. She kept her accounts with the utmost care and was described as "an elegant and aristocratic lady who always wore a white turban after the fashion of the famous Dolley Madison." In 1845, and very likely later, Mrs. Gray was still operating Hotel E so successfully that no one thought of calling it anything but "Mrs. Gray's hotel."

As the student body grew, it was inevitable that Jefferson's arrangement of separate dining halls should become inadequate. In the 1880s only two hotels, A and E, operated as such. By 1916 the Jeffersonian part of Hotel E, together with several adjacent student rooms had become a faculty residence. In 1919, when a class of six students assembled under Professor Fiske Kimball in an upstairs room of the addition to Hotel E, the university's formal curriculum in architecture began, although courses in drawing and construction had been taught as early as 1832. The annex also was used for classes and meetings by the Department of Speech and Drama. In the 1930s, forty years before undergraduate female students were admitted to the university, a "Coed Room" fitted as a lounge was opened on the ground floor of the annex; in 1953 a second-floor room was designated the Graduate Students' Center. In the 1980s Hotel E is the only one of the hotels where meals are still served.

To enter the garden of Pavilion IX, the visitor turns right at the first gate in the long brick wall between the gardens and the walk behind Hotel E.

In 1948 the Garden Club of Virginia began allocating the proceeds from its Historic Garden Week to the gardens of the West Lawn pavilions, as designed by Alden Hopkins. Much planning went into determining the characteristics each garden should display. Service buildings and dependencies were removed, and rubble was cleared away. Walls were restored to the positions shown on the Maverick Plan. As

walks, gates, and steps were repaired or replaced, the gardens began to assume the kind of appearance it was believed Jefferson intended. By 1952 the restoration, reconstruction, and planting of the West Lawn gardens were completed, and on April 24 the Garden Club presented the project as a gift to the university.

The outer section of Pavilion IX's divided garden was once the house garden for Hotel E. A small allée of dwarf apples borders a straight gravel path flanked by rectangles of grass outlined in walks. The allée ends at a white trellis bench against the dividing serpentine wall. There are two small pomegranate trees beside the north serpentine wall. The only other plantings are a large magnolia and a large white ash, both casually placed for shade.

A two-panel lattice gate leads into the pavilion or family garden. Here the ground pattern is in curved lines and circles, as the walk from the gate bends inward. The flower beds against the dividing serpentine wall have serpentine borders. All is molded to complement the dominating McGuffey Ash, which stands majestically in a ground-cover bed against the Colonnade Alley wall. The garden's open grassy center is outlined in beds of spring and summer flowers—iris, lilies, geraniums, phlox—and by common box and perennials.

Crossing the back of Pavilion IX against a brick addition in common bond of about 1860 are two later long-roofed porches, one above the other, overlooking the garden. A small wing near McGuffey Cottage also was added to the house in the nineteenth century to provide a new dining room. Its interior was modeled on the tearoom at Monticello.

THE GARDEN OF PAVILION VII

Outside the outer garden of Pavilion IX, locust and honey locust trees overhang the long walk. High common box screen the windows of the West Range student rooms. Across Colonnade Alley, farther up the walk, on the left is another iron Corinthian capital from the Rotunda Annex, a relic from the 1895 fire. A third such capital stands on the front terrace of the university's art museum, the Bayly Museum on Rugby Road.

An unobtrusive white gate on the right, in one corner of Pavilion VII's garden wall, leads into a leafy nook with bench and chairs. This is one of four such sitting corners. Because this is the Colonnade Club's garden, it was designed for outdoor entertaining. The plan of this garden was adopted from Georges Louis Le Rouge's *Jardins Anglo-Chinois* of 1785. It repeats a circular motif in each corner and in the large center disk. Here a greensward encircled by a walk creates space for large gatherings, and the triangular corners on the outer side of the walk are suitable for intimate little groups. From the pavilion the garden is reached by wide brick steps leading down from a long, arbored terrace outside the reading room. Above the pergola, the fanlight in the rear pediment of the two-story addition repeats the Jeffersonian motif from the front pediment.

In the four small corner retreats, beds of English ivy and periwinkle behind shrubs provide a year-round ground cover. In the spring bulbs bloom in clusters—jonquils, daffodils, hyacinths, anemones, and tulips. As the years pass, these are replaced, although not always in kind. The shrubs are lilac, holly, nandina, and oakleaf hydrangea.

The low trees are American hollies, redbud, and dogwood. Overhead are large magnolias. Red maples have recently been planted here to replace some ancient mulberry trees. For evening entertaining, there are lights in some of the larger trees.

Because it has more benches and chairs than any other garden, Pavilion VII's garden attracts more lingering visitors, and there is no prohibition here against moving the garden furniture.

WOODROW WILSON'S ROOM

From the garden of Pavilion VII, north on the long walk to Patterson Alley, named for the second occupant of Pavilion V, Professor Robert M. Patterson, Room 31 of the West Range can be reached by turning left and ascending six steps under the arcade. It is the second bottle-green door on the left.

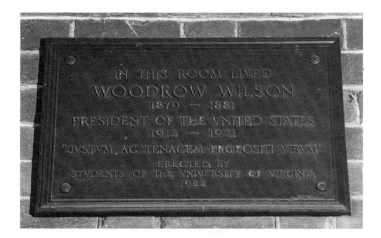

Over the six-panel door and its screened double louvers, a bronze plaque explains that between 1879 and 1881 Woodrow Wilson lived here as a student.

Twenty-one years after leaving, Wilson declined the first offer of the new presidency of the university. The plaque was placed by students in 1922, shortly after he ended his second term as president of the United States. The room is assigned to a student as any other room.

Across Patterson Alley, north under the arcade is Hotel C.

HOTEL C

Hotel C, long called "Jeff Hall" by students, is a one-story pedimented brick building behind a triple-arch arcade. It retains its double front doors with bottle-green paint. On the right-hand door a modest brass tablet reading "JEFFERSON SOCIETY 1825" marks this building as the home of the venerable student oratorical and debating club. "The Jeff" proudly claims to be "the oldest functioning collegiate literary society in the nation." Although it came into being in Room 7, West Lawn, on Thursday, July 14, 1825, it has met continuously since 1826 in Hotel C and currrently meets on Fridays at 7:29 P.M. It was founded by sixteen members of

the Patrick Henry Society who were dissatisfied with the disorder at meetings. The Patrick Henry did not survive.

Although Jefferson in 1825 declined honorary membership because of his position as university rector, Madison, Monroe, and Lafayette accepted. Woodrow Wilson once served as the society's president. Poe was elected an active member on June 17, 1826. As required, he soon read an essay of his own, on the subject of "Heat and Cold." He debated once or twice and once acted as secretary pro tempore. As the price of his fame, a curio thief years ago cut his signature from the minute book.

Social events were soon vying with the forensic and literary exercises in Jefferson Hall; student dances began to be given here in the late 1820s. On October 14, 1829, the student boarders in Mrs. Gray's hotel gave a ball for about 100 persons in the then unoccupied Hotel C. Both the reel and waltz were danced. Faculty permission for this ball was granted on condition that it end by midnight and that it cost each student, including wine and supper, no more than $1.50. Fiddle music was provided by black Jesse Scott and his son. So successful was this ball that for years afterward the various hotels held such fetes.

When early student enrollment did not support use of all hotels as dining halls, Hotel C was put to various uses. In 1833 Louis Carusi began teaching fencing and dancing here. He was succeeded by Major Penci, who taught fencing and gymnastics in this hotel.

Since its founding in 1904, the Raven Society also has held occasional meetings in Jeff Hall. Taking its name from Poe's most famous poem, the society brings together exceptionally outstanding students—undergraduate, graduate, and professional—in the various schools, together with members of the faculty and alumni, in order to sustain the university's honor and dignity, to advance its welfare and interests, to encourage diligent scholarship, and to stimulate continuous intellectual activity beyond the classroom. It elects student members only one year before their graduation. Among its first alumni members were Thomas Nelson Page, author and diplomat, and Woodrow Wilson. Membership in the Raven Society is recognized as one of the most significant honors at the university.

In keeping with its long tradition, "the Jeff" still maintains an outside bulletin board on the wall between Jefferson Hall and student room No. 23 West Range. Under the arcade, basement half-windows reveal the onetime location of the hotel's kitchen and dining area.

THE GARDEN OF PAVILION V

From the long walk directly behind Hotel C, opposite the entrance to a present-day bathroom in its basement for West Range students, is a white trellis gate of fretwork in diamond patterns. This gate leads into the outer garden of Pavilion V, the most open and formally stylized of all the Lawn gardens.

The use of brick-edged, gravel-walk parterres set in grass creates a French mood. The quadrants are centered on two gravel circles. In the center of each stands a large Albemarle pippin tree, known locally as the "royal apple," because its fruit was Queen Victoria's favorite and a county orchard sent it to her annually.

This garden is sometimes chosen as the one to be illuminated during the annual springtime "Lawn Tours by Candlelight." On that evening, its geometric design is outlined by scores of luminarias—candles set in sand in brown paper bags on the ground—lighting the borders of its walks.

Beyond it, through the white gate in the center dividing serpentine wall, the garden that is overlooked by Pavilion V, Poe Alley presents a striking contrast. It is as closed in mood as the outer garden is exposed. Narrow walks wind in a maze of English box, bordered by sweeping beds of hosta that lift their blue spike-blooms in midsummer. Two of its three serpentine walls are bordered by crape myrtles. In the spring cherry trees against the Poe Alley wall set up a screen of white blossoms. Low pieces of statuary stand at unexpected places in the box.

This garden is shaded by a willow oak and two gigantic coffee trees. In the greenery two white lattice benches are almost obscured. Even the pavilion's long roofed veranda does not obtrude upon the tranquillity of this serene and beautiful green-garden. Its width permits an entrance to it from the top of Patterson Alley and another from the top of Poe Alley.

EDGAR ALLAN POE'S ROOM

Outside the outer garden of Pavilion V is a large old Norway spruce with branches touching the ground at the corner of Poe Alley. To the left here and then to the right under the arcade is room No. 13 on the West Range, the second door on the right. This was Edgar Allan Poe's residence when he was a student. Above the door is a bronze plaque bearing his name, the date of his school year, 1826, and the words "DOMUS PARVA MAGNI POETAE."

The room was furnished by the Raven Society in 1930 with simple furniture. In 1942, under Professor Edmund S.

Campbell of the School of Architecture, the room was refurnished to reproduce, as nearly as possible, Poe's room. By adding sand to putty-colored paint, Campbell had the wooden door casings of all the student rooms restored to the imitation stone finish Jefferson had given them. In 1956 room No. 13 was rehabilitated to its original appearance: a modern door was replaced with an old one from No. 49 West Range, iron louvered-door latches from No. 51 were installed, and the hearth was rebuilt in Jeffersonian brick from the demolished Anatomical Theater. Twin cupboards and a mantel, all of a later date, were removed, and original window glass was found to replace newer panes. In 1979, through the generosity of several friends of the university, the Poe Room was again refurnished, in observation of the seventy-fifth anniversary of the Raven Society.

Poe entered the university on February 14, 1826, at age seventeen. Having already studied Latin and French in England and Richmond, he enrolled in both the School of Ancient Languages and that of Modern Languages. He was, thus, a pupil of Professor Long in Pavilion V and Professor Blaettermann in Pavilion IV. He had classes from 7:30 to 9:30 A.M. six days a week, and in his final examinations he excelled in both Latin and French.

When Poe moved into No. 13 West Range, that block was already known as "Rowdy Row." Here he began to play cards and to experiment with "peach and honey," as homemade peach brandy was called. However, he also checked out of the library various histories and other books in French and was never in conflict with the university authorities. His fellow students recalled that Poe "delighted and entertained" his friends by reading his own poems; students often filled his room and "scarcely breathed as they eagerly listened to some story" he had written. It is almost certain that he wrote his 400-line poem "Tamerlane" in Room 13, as well as other poems in his first volume, published in the spring of 1827 when he was eighteen and walking the streets of Boston.

His one academic year at the University of Virginia ended in December 1826. Two of his stories, "William Wilson" (1839) and "A Tale of the Ragged Mountains" (1844) reflect aspects of his life at the university.

Each year in October the University Guide Service stages a Poe weekend, when his room is opened to the public.

THE GARDEN OF PAVILION III

From Poe's room back by Poe Alley to the long walk and north is the gate to the long garden of Pavilion III. This is the smallest garden on the Lawn. A large deodar in the entrance corner partially shades a green island of ligustrum growing in beds of ivy. It is bordered with an elliptical gravel walk that leads to the periphery of the garden. Just inside the gate wall there is an enormous Biltmore white ash. A similar ash overhangs the Poe Alley wall. Near it are a Carolina silverbell tree, a distant relative of the tea plant which is native to the Carolinas, and a large Kentucky coffee tree.

The sweeping greensward in the center of the garden rises upward in a long vista to the house. Two walks gently follow a serpentine line as they weave against the center lawn on both sides. At the top, the garden is narrowed on the right by the small administrative building seen earlier from Poe Alley and on the left by a small two-story brick house set in its own walled garden. Both are so carefully screened by planting as to be almost unobserved. The latter building, though once variously servants' quarters, a washhouse, and a chicken house for Pavilion III, now enjoys the status of a Lawn residence and is known as the Mews. It is entered from Mews Alley on its north or outer side and contains a separate apartment on each floor.

Although no outside porch or paved terrace has been added to Pavilion III, it does have an outside back entrance with steps leading up to it. Entrance from the parking places in Poe Alley is through a small area at the top of the garden, set off by common boxwood. Because of the rising ridge on which the Lawn is placed, the two-and-one-half-story back wall of the pavilion is visible from the garden. The pavilion's small pediment contains a fanlight.

In this garden's lower center is a weathered Ionic capital of native stone, one of the rejects Jefferson found unsuitable for Lawn portico columns. In the corner formed by the gate wall and the Mews Alley wall, three deodar trees stand. Dogwoods, hollies, oakleaf hydrangeas, and a small native viburnum complete the garden's planting. Midway up the center sweep, two white benches, visible in the greenery, face each other across the open.

THE GARDEN OF PAVILION I

From the Pavilion III garden, the long back walk continues across Mews Alley, where a glance to the right shows that this alley has no opening to the Lawn. To the left is one side of Hotel A; because of the ground fall from the Rotunda, two stories of the hotel are visible here.

Hotel A's former basement kitchen is now occupied by offices. Growing on the walled-in basement level, a large weeping willow rises to overhang a part of the hotel roof and the walk to Pavilion I's lower garden. Behind the hotel, the walk is supported by a heavy stone wall.

At the northwest corner of Pavilion I's garden, where the back wall joins the side serpentine wall, is a white gate with diamond fretwork leading into the last of the Lawn gardens. This garden makes its best appearance briefly in the spring, when its three-sided border of pink flowering crab-apple trees is in bloom. Its grassy center is spaced in rectangles set in right-angle walks.

There is a louvered necessary to the left built into the outer wall. With the usual two doors in the lower garden and two in the upper, it is now a toolshed. Up three steps in front of it in the dividing serpentine wall is a gate of solid white panels leading into the upper garden. The theme here is white flowering plants. The sharp fall of the land exposes all

three stories of Pavilion I. Across its back, the width of the house, stretches a brick addition of the 1850s.

Outside the addition, a broad brick and gravel terrace provides space for dining and recreation. There is no porch; access to the house is at ground level. Against the house are two Washington hawthorns. There is an outside gate on each side of the upper garden. The rest of the garden consists of a grass plot bordered with curving walks and outlined in white azaleas and flower beds. In the center of the grass is a rejected capital of Virginia stone on which carving was barely begun. A white trellis bench stands against the outside serpentine wall. Across the garden are two large photinias, broadleaf evergreens, against the Mews Alley wall, and a large willow oak overhangs the alley and its entrance gate.

Outside the lower garden of Pavilion I, on its back wall, is a plaque noting that the walls were designed and first built by Thomas Jefferson in 1821–24 and that the West Lawn gardens, as now constituted and restored in 1952, were designed by Alden Hopkins.

137

HOTEL A

Across from the plaque is Hotel A, at the north end of the West Range. This low brick building, repaired after it burned in 1923, was restored in 1966 to its original form. It has a metal roof without the usual stand-up seams. Its one-story, four-columned Doric portico lends imposing dignity to the building; unlike the portico of Hotel B, it is shown on the Maverick Plan. Superb English box flank the main entrance. There is another entrance under the West Range arcade.

As one of the last two of Jefferson's refectories to function as a dining facility, Hotel A reached its peak in the late nineteenth century when it was called Elsom's Boarding House, serving faculty meals only. Students had their own separate dining hall in a large brick building next door, where Pavilion I's restored gardens now are. With the Rotunda Annex and its public hall so near, this concentration of activities was considered the height of convenience. After the Rotunda fire and the removal of classes to the south end of the Lawn, the student dining hall was razed after 1907. At one time Hotel A was the Physiology Laboratory. Since 1928 the editorial offices of the *Virginia Quarterly Review* have occupied it.

The tour ends at this point back at the chapel bus stop. Jefferson's buildings at the University of Virginia are mankind's greatest monument to the Enlightenment. As that eighteenth-century movement utilized human reason to increase man's knowledge of himself and the world around him, so this university is fulfilling its rightful and continuing place in the ever-growing universe of knowledge.

SELECTED BIBLIOGRAPHY

Abernethy, Thomas Perkins. *Historical Sketch of the University of Virginia*. Richmond: Dietz Press, 1948.

Adams, Herbert Baxter, *Thomas Jefferson and the University of Virginia*. U.S. Bureau of Education, Circular of Information no. 1. Washington, D.C.: GPO, 1888.

Adams, William Howard, ed. *The Eye of Thomas Jefferson*. Charlottesville: University Press of Virginia, 1981.

Barrett, Clifton Waller. "The Struggle to Create a University." *Virginia Quarterly Review* 49(Autumn 1973): 494–506.

Barringer, Anna. "Pleasant It Is to Remember These Things." *Magazine of Albemarle County History* 24(1965–66): 5–38, 27 (1968–69): 5–116.

Barringer, Paul Brandon, James Mercer Garnett, and Rosewell Page. *University of Virginia*. 2 vols. New York: Lewis Publishing Company, 1904.

Bowers, Claude G. *The Young Jefferson, 1743–1789*. Boston: Houghton Mifflin Company, 1945.

Brockenbrough, Arthur S. Proctor's Journal, 1819–28. Manuscripts Department, University of Virginia Library.

Bruce, Philip Alexander. *History of the University of Virginia, 1819–1919*. 5 vols. New York: Macmillan, 1922.

Childress, Mark. "The Idea That Jefferson Built." *Southern Living* 16(Sept. 1981): 36–39.

Clark, Margaret W. Fowler. "Facts Relating to the Surrender of Charlottesville, March 3, 1865." *Magazine of Albemarle County History* 17(1958–59): 67–73.

Crawford, Benjamin Franklin. *W. H. McGuffey*. Delaware, Ohio: Carnegie Church Press, 1974.

Cruse, Kathy, and Barbara Wartelle. "Mr. Jefferson's Architecture." *Cavalier Daily* (University of Virginia), Oct. 16–Nov. 15, 1974. Ten articles, one on each pavilion.

Culbreth, David M. R. *The University of Virginia: Memories of Her Student-Life and Professors*. New York and Washington, D.C.: Neale Publishing Co., 1908.

Dabney, Virginius. *Mr. Jefferson's University.* Charlottesville: University Press of Virginia, 1981.

Dumbauld, Edward. *Thomas Jefferson, American Tourist.* Norman: University of Oklahoma Press, 1976.

Dunnington, Bell. Letter, Oct. 28, 1895. Manuscripts Department, University of Virginia Library.

Eddins, Joe. *Around the Corner after World War I.* Charlottesville: Published by the author, 1973.

Foster, Joseph Arnold, ed. *Accounts of Brickmaking in America Written before 1850.* Claremont, Calif.: Privately printed, 1960.

Goode, James M., "'Old Guff' in Virginia." *Virginia Cavalcade* 16 (Summer 1966): 4–9.

Hubbard, William. "The Meaning of Buildings." Review of *American Architecture, 1607–1976,* by Marcus Whiffen and Frederick Koeper. *New Republic* 185(Nov. 18, 1981): 27–31.

Huxtable, Ada Louise. "Noted Architecture Critic Praises Buildings at University of Virginia." *Richmond Times-Dispatch,* March 9, 1975, Section D, pp. 1–2.

Jefferson, Thomas. *Notes on the State of Virginia.* Ed. William H. Peden. Chapel Hill: University of North Carolina Press, 1955.

"Jefferson Statue by Moses Ezekiel." *University of Virginia Alumni Bulletin* 3, no. 2 (1910): 191–92.

Kimball, Fiske. "The Genius of Jefferson's Plan for the University of Virginia." *Professional Architectural Monthly* 48, no. 6 (Dec. 1924): 397–99.

———. *Thomas Jefferson, Architect.* With new introduction by Frederick D. Nichols. New York: Da Capo Press, 1968.

———. "Jefferson and the Public Buildings of Virginia, Part 1; Williamsburg, 1770–76." *Huntington Library Quarterly* 12, no. 2 (Feb. 1949): 115–20.

Lambeth, William Alexander, and Warren Henry Manning. *Thomas Jefferson as an Architect and Designer of Landscapes.* Boston: Houghton Mifflin, 1913.

Malone, Dumas. *Jefferson and His Time.* 6 vols. Boston: Little, Brown, 1948–81.

Manual of the Board of Visitors of the University of Virginia, 1975.

Mayo, Bernard, *Jefferson Himself.* 1942; rept. Charlottesville: University Press of Virginia, 1970.

———. *Another Peppercorn for Mr. Jefferson.* Speech given at fall convocation, University of Virginia, Charlottesville, Oct. 15, 1976.

Charlottesville: Thomas Jefferson Memorial Foundation, 1977.

Minutes of the Faculty of the University of Virginia. Vols. 1 and 2, April 12, 1825–July 16, 1830. Manuscripts Department, University of Virginia Library.

Minutes of the Rectors and Visitors of the University of Virginia. Vol. 1, 1825–28. Manuscripts Department, University of Virginia Library.

Murphy, Anna Marie and Cullen. "Onward, Upward with Those Readers." *Smithsonian Magazine* 15, no. 8 (Nov. 1984): 182–208.

Nichols, Frederick Doveton. "A Day to Remember: The Burning of the Rotunda, 1895." *Magazine of Albemarle County History* 17(1958–59): 57–65.

———. *Thomas Jefferson's Architectural Drawings.* 1960; 4th ed., rev. and enl., Boston: Massachusetts Historical Society and Charlottesville: Thomas Jefferson Memorial Foundation and the University Press of Virginia, 1978.

———, and James A. Bear, Jr. *Monticello, a Guidebook.* 2d ed., Monticello, Va.: Thomas Jefferson Memorial Foundation, 1982.

———, and Ralph E. Griswold. *Thomas Jefferson: Landscape Architect.* Charlottesville: University Press of Virginia, 1978.

O'Neal, William B. *Architecture in Virginia: An Official Guide to Four Centuries of Building in the Old Dominion.* New York: Walker and Company for the Virginia Museum, 1968.

———. *Jefferson's Buildings at the University of Virginia: The Rotunda.* Charlottesville: University of Virginia Press, 1960.

———. *Jefferson's Fine Arts Library: His Selections for the University of Virginia, Together with His Own Architectural Books.* Charlottesville: University Press of Virginia, 1976.

———. *Pictorial History of the University of Virginia.* 2d ed. Charlottesville: University Press of Virginia, 1980.

———. "Workmen at the University of Virginia, 1817–1826." *Magazine of Albemarle County History* 17(1958–59): 5–16.

Patton, John S., and Sallie J. Doswell. *The University of Virginia: Glimpses of Its Past and Present.* Lynchburg, Va.: J. P. Bell Company, 1900.

Settle, Mary Lee. "Mr. Jefferson's World." *New York Times Magazine,* March 13, 1983, pt. 2, pp. 122–28.

Shawen, Neil McDowell. "The Casting of a Lengthened Shadow:

Thomas Jefferson's Role in Determining the Site for a State
University in Virginia." Ph.D. diss., George Washington University, 1980.

Thurlow, Constance E., et al., comps. *The Jefferson Papers of the University of Virginia.* Charlottesville: Published for the University of Virginia Library by the University Press of Virginia, 1973.

University of Virginia, Office of Sports Information. *The University.* 1981. Media guide.

University of Virginia, Student Guide Services. *Rotunda Manual.* 1982.

"The University of Virginia: Thomas Jefferson's Academical Village." *University of Virginia Record,* 1982–83, pp. 3–5.

Vaughan, Joseph Lee, and Omer Allan Gianniny. *Thomas Jefferson's Rotunda Restored.* Charlottesville: University Press of Virginia, 1981.

Wilkerson, Elizabeth. *Mr. Jefferson's Rotunda: A Return to the Original.* Pamphlet, rept. from *University of Virginia Alumni News,* Jan.–Feb. 1976.

Williams, Dorothy Hunt. *Historic Virginia Gardens.* Charlottesville: Published for the Garden Club of Virginia by the University Press of Virginia, 1975.

Wilson, Richard Guy. "The French Architectural Connection." *Daily Progress,* Sept. 21, 1982, CHALFA's "Our Community and the Arts" supplement, p. 19.

INDEX

144

145

147

VISITOR INFORMATION

The Rotunda is open seven days a week from 9:00 A.M. to 4:45 P.M. except during Christmas break (mid-December to mid-January).

Parking: metered parking is provided at Memorial Gym parking lot on Emmet Street (Rt. 29) below Newcomb Hall and across Emmet Street at Ruffner Hall.

Temporary University Transit Service bus passes and parking permits for a three-day minimum may be purchased at the University Department of Parking and Transportation, 1101 Millmont Street, the first street behind Barracks Road Shopping Center on Rt. 29 N. This office also makes arrangements for large groups to park when visiting the Lawn (804-924-7231).

Tours: The University Guide Service, a volunteer student organization, conducts free tours of the Lawn every day throughout the year at 10 and 11 A.M. and 2, 3, and 4 P.M. The tours begin in the Rotunda and last about one hour. Special historical tours for groups may be booked in advance by calling the Rotunda at 804-924-7969.

Admission Tours for prospective students are conducted by the Office of Admissions throughout the year, except for certain student vacation periods, on Monday through Friday at 11:00 and 2:00 P.M. and on Saturday mornings at 11:00. Write or call the Office of Admissions, University of Virginia, P.O. Box 9017, Charlottesville, Virginia, 22906, telephone 804-924-7751.

Signs on roads to Charlottesville direct the traveler to the University of Virginia Visitors Center, at the University Police Dept. on Rt. 250W, off the Rt. 29 bypass. The center is open 24 hours every day and provides general area information and maps (804-924-7166).

THE LAWN

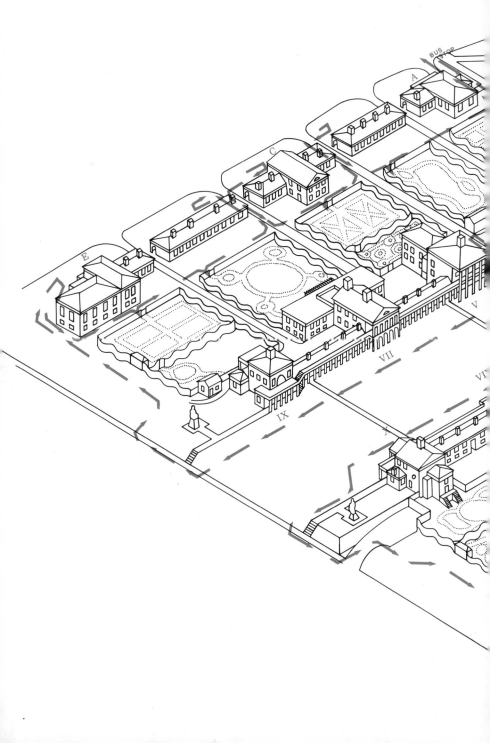